Distinctive Qualiti
Research

This timely volume provides an in-depth look at why the field of communication is so central in initiatives for social impact around the world. In *Distinctive Qualities in Communication Research*, editors Donal Carbaugh and Patrice M. Buzzanell bring together scholars with varied and productive approaches to communication to address the question of what distinguishes communication research from similar studies in other disciplines. Each contributor responds to the questions: "What makes your research *communication* research? How does your program of inquiry treat communication not simply as data, but as its primary theoretical concern?" Their responses are the heart of this book.

The questions addressed and answered herein define the qualities that set research in communication apart from work in related fields, such as social psychology, linguistics, sociology, anthropology, and psychology. The book begins and ends by looking across these studies generally, bringing into view not only the specific possibilities in the study of communication today, but also what such study contributes generally to understanding human problems, social relations, and communities.

This volume provides an invaluable resource for graduate students beginning their study in communication; academics needing to define the distinctive contributions that communication research makes; and administrators who want to understand the scope and breadth of work in communication. It serves to articulate the role of communication research in the academic community and the contributions it makes to the study of human interaction.

About the Editors

Donal Carbaugh is Professor of Communication and Chair of the International Studies Council (2004–present) at the University of

Massachusetts, Amherst. His most recent book, *Cultures in Conversation*, was designated the Outstanding Book of the Year by the International and Intercultural Communication Division of the National Communication Association. Focusing on indigenous, environmental, and cultural issues, he has served as Fulbright's Distinguished Professor and Bicentennial Chair at the University of Helsinki, Finland, and has enjoyed lecturing about the distinctive qualities of communication research around the world.

Patrice M. Buzzanell is Professor and the W. Charles and Ann Redding Faculty Fellow in the Department of Communication at Purdue University. Her primary interest is in organizational communication, specializing in career, leadership, and work-life issues. Recipient of numerous research, teaching, mentoring, and service awards including NCA's Francine Merritt Award and OSCLG's Teacher-Mentor Award, Buzzanell is President of the International Communication Association and President of the Council of Communication Associations. She teaches in Purdue's Engineering Projects in Community Service (EPICS) program and currently serves on 13 editorial boards.

Distinctive Qualities in Communication Research

Edited by

**Donal Carbaugh and
Patrice M. Buzzanell**

Routledge
Taylor & Francis Group

NEW YORK AND LONDON

First published 2010
by Routledge
270 Madison Ave, New York, NY 10016

Simultaneously published in the UK
by Routledge
2 Park Square, Milton Park, Abingdon, Oxon OX14 4RN

Routledge is an imprint of the Taylor & Francis Group, an informa business

© 2010 Taylor & Francis

Typeset in Minion by
RefineCatch Limited, Bungay, Suffolk
Printed and bound in the United States of America on acid-free paper by
Walsworth Publishing Company, Marceline, MO

Library of Congress Cataloging-in-Publication Data
   Distinctive qualities in communication research / edited by Donal Carbaugh and Patrice Buzzanell.
     p. cm.
   Includes bibliographical references and index.
     ISBN 978–0–415–99025–7—ISBN 978–0–415–99026–4   1. Communication—Research. I. Carbaugh, Donal A. II. Buzzanell, Patrice M.
     P91.3.D57 2009
   302.207′2—dc22
   2008055476

ISBN10: 0–415–99025–4 (hbk)
ISBN10: 0–415–99026–2 (pbk)
ISBN10: 0–203–87416–1 (ebk)

ISBN13: 978–0–415–99025–7 (hbk)
ISBN13: 978–0–415–99026–4 (pbk)
ISBN13: 978–0–203–87416–5 (ebk)

CONTENTS

FOREWORD

Robert T. Craig

Plato's dialogue *Gorgias* portrays an exchange between the philosopher Socrates and Gorgias, a notable sophist or popular teacher, concerning the distinctive qualities of rhetoric, a field of study that is surely the oldest tradition of communication research (see the selections from Plato and Aristotle in Craig & Muller, 2007, pp. 107–130). Asked by Socrates to name the subject matter of rhetoric, Gorgias initially replies that it is discourse. Socratic follow-up questions soon reveal the inadequacy of this answer. Aren't all arts concerned with discourse on their respective subject matters—medicine on sickness and health, gymnastics on the condition of the body, and so forth? Yes. Should all of them be called arts of rhetoric, then? No, of course not, says Gorgias, but these other arts all involve actions of the hand while rhetoric relies entirely on discourse. Socrates asks, but what about arithmetic and other arts that work entirely through the medium of language? Since these all are arts of discourse but, as Gorgias admits, not forms of rhetoric, the distinctive quality of rhetoric must lie in the specific end that it serves. Medicine produces health. Arithmetic produces calcula-tions. What does rhetoric produce? Socrates and Gorgias quickly agree that it produces persuasion, but persuasion about what? Don't teachers in every field persuade us about the things they know? Doctors are the ones most qualified to persuade on matters of health; craftsmen, on matters of shipbuilding. What about rhetoricians? On what are they most qualified to persuade? Gorgias argues that a skilled rhetorician can persuade the public on any subject whatever. The rhetorician, not the doctor, is better able to persuade patients to take their medicine.

Rhetoricians, not craftsmen, actually persuade the public to build ships. Skill in rhetoric confers power over specialized knowledge. Further questioning of Gorgias on the implications of this argument finally leads Socrates to the rather disheartening (to a rhetorician) conclusion that rhetoric is not a legitimate art at all. Rhetoricians have no distinct knowledge of their own; what they have, at best, is a kind of knack for persuading ignorant people to believe things that may or may not be true.

Some twenty-four centuries later, and in quite different circumstances, the distinctive qualities of communication research are once again in question, and the ancient Greek debate on the art of rhetoric continues to be instructive. In a later dialogue, *Phaedrus*, Plato envisioned an ideal rhetoric that would be a legitimate art if it were to meet two requirements. First, the rhetorician must always ascertain the philosophical truth on any subject (through dialectic) before inspiring an audience to believe that truth (through rhetoric). Second, the practice of rhetoric must be based on genuine knowledge of the psychological principles by which persuasion occurs—a theory of the different kinds of souls and how each kind can best be moved by the use of rhetoric. Plato did not address the practical problems involved in meeting these requirements. Doctors and craftsmen presumably would continue to be the only true experts in their respective fields. The ideal rhetorician, as well as being skilled in speaking, must be an expert on psychology and also on any topic about which she might choose to speak. Since no one could really do all of this, rhetoricians must either become narrow specialists in other fields or else distinctly subordinate members of what we would call interdisciplinary teams. Rhetoric still would not be viable as an independent art or discipline.

Plato's less idealistic successor, Aristotle, took a different approach. A distinct art of rhetoric, he argued, is both possible and ethically legitimate. Among rhetoric's distinctive qualities are that it is a *techne* or productive art of discovering the means of persuasion in particular situations and that it is concerned with matters of general interest rather than any specialized field of knowledge. Rhetoric can develop a distinctive kind of theory by investigating the practice of successful speakers. Rhetoric is justified ethically on pragmatic grounds, because there is no other way to participate effectively in popular debates on questions of common concern about which opinions are divided and no definitive scientific answer is possible (such as a decision about going to war). Aristotle warned that rhetoricians tend to masquerade as experts, such as political scientists, and that they must keep in mind that their art is restricted to popular opinion, not scientific knowledge.

He did not tell us precisely where to draw this important line, however, or what do about issues that seem to straddle it.

The ancient question of rhetoric's legitimacy is instructive both for how it resembles and how it differs from present concerns about the distinctiveness of communication research. The present field, of course, is broader, more diverse, and more methodologically sophisticated than ancient rhetoric, and our modern concept of an academic discipline is substantially different, yet the problem of distinctiveness is similar in at least one important way. Whether we think of communication as a technical process of transmitting messages or as a constitutive social practice of negotiating meaning, communication is, like rhetoric, a universal process or practice that encompasses many different topics (health, nanotechnology), contexts (politics, marriage), influences (emotion, culture), and means (language, information technology), all of which are studied by other specialized disciplines. Are there specific kinds of communication knowledge that are somehow applicable across topics and contexts and distinguishable from all of these other fields of expertise? Is communication a discipline, an interdisciplinary field, or a topic that just happens to be studied in various disciplines and fields? Could it be all three? What, in short, are the distinctive qualities of communication research?

An approach to this question must begin with the realization that modern academic disciplines do not correspond neatly to conceptually defined categories of knowledge. Disciplines differ from each other in numerous ways, but there is little sense in asking, as Plato would, for example, what is the unchanging *essence* of communication research that forever distinguishes it from biology or economics. There is no such essence, and yet there are clearly differences. Disciplines are better described as complex, evolving nexuses of intellectual traditions and trends, institutional–professional politics, and interactions with the wider society and culture (Craig, 2008). Disciplines are internally fragmented and contentious, overlap broadly, and borrow shamelessly from one another. The most exciting research often occurs in-between or outside of established disciplines. Yet these invigorating impulses toward interdisciplinary openness and innovation are in tension with other forces that impel scholars to define standards of disciplinary rigor and specialized expertise. And so, the question of defining a discipline cannot be avoided for practical purposes, the meta-conversation must go on, even though it can lead to no final consensus.

Distinctive Qualities in Communication Research, edited by Donal Carbaugh and Patrice M. Buzzanell, is a timely and useful contribution to the meta-conversation about communication research. Five central chapters by leading communication researchers present diverse views of the field that are deeply rooted in their particular methodological approaches, research programs, and institutional positions. Opening and closing chapters by the editors move the conversation forward, highlighting common themes as well as differences among the chapters. Several chapters reflect on the distinct contributions of communication research to large-scale funded research projects and/or interdisciplinary teams. Several chapters also reflect on the meaning of a distinct communication perspective toward the world and the practical implications, whether ethical or methodological, of adopting such a perspective.

If terms like message, discourse, process, content, and communication practice all refer to aspects of an underlying something that might also be called *actual communication*, then the following chapters display a striking consensus that a distinctive quality of communication research—perhaps the field's most distinctive quality—is that it tends to focus on that something. I would hazard to add that our focus on that something also tends to have a distinctive *practical* quality, an orientation to the activities of everyday people communicating in ordinary situations for ordinary purposes. This focus is not inconsistent with the use of sophisticated theories and research methodologies, but the departure points and ultimate goals of communication research tend to lie in the commonplace—in actual communication for the sake of managing interpersonal problems, making decisions in groups, or encountering cultural differences.

Even when we collaborate with experts in medicine and public health or study technical talk among nanoscientists, the distinctive contribution of communication research tends to involve connecting those expert perspectives with the perspectives of ordinary people as members of audiences, cultures, or publics. For example, communication research on talk among nanoscientists speaks to the general public's interest in the social and ethical implications of nanoscience, not to the technical problems of nanoscience proper (see Philipsen, Chapter 6 in this volume). We are, after all, communication researchers, not nanoscientists or medical doctors. Our purview, like that of the ancient rhetoricians, extends not too far from the commonplace.

REFERENCES

Craig, R. T. (2008). Communication in the conversation of disciplines. *Russian Journal of Communication, 1*, 7–23.

Craig, R. T., & Muller, H. L. (Eds.). (2007). *Theorizing communication: Readings across traditions.* Thousand Oaks, CA: Sage.

ACKNOWLEDGMENTS

This collection began with our participation on the National Communication Association Research Board (NCA RB). On the Research Board, our task was to represent our discipline and its research to various audiences and agencies, and we did so in conjunction with other associations dedicated to particular aspects of our field, such as the International Communication Association (ICA) and the Council of Communication Associations (CCA, which includes eight associations representing such areas as business communication, broadcast education, journalism and mediated communication, and Black College Communication Association issues, see http://www.councilcomm.org).

In promoting this collective mission of facilitating research and representing our field, we brought together the prominent group of communication scholars whose work is assembled here onto an NCA panel in 2006 in San Antonio, Texas. The panel was designed, like this book, to address the uniqueness of each approach to the study of communication. The original panel was composed of six scholars representing different theoretical stances, focused on different communication contexts, engaged in productive research programs, in various institutions of higher education, with a wide range of administrative and editorial backgrounds, and funding experiences. Five of these same scholars agreed to submit an essay to this collection.[1] Their essays form the substantive chapters in this book and provide a basis for engaging in dialogue about the current status of research in the field of communication as well as its future possibilities.

We dedicate this book to the people most important in our lives—our families.

NOTE

1. We regret that Judee Burgoon (University of Arizona) was unable to participate in this edited collection but we are grateful for her contributions to our NCA panel. In her address, Judee articulated a challenge for the intellectual respectability and identity of the field. Instead of being associated with the practical disciplines (i.e., skills-oriented fields or professional schools), Communication is sometimes known as a "service department" rather than a research center. As a result, departments of communication may operate in academic arenas with less force. She recommended that communication specialists are, and need to increasingly be, at the table for funding initiatives. They need to insure that research projects incorporate communication as a dynamic process that has an impact on the ways that real-world problems are discussed and solved. In particular, from her view, the unique aspects in communication studies are researchers' investigations of the messages themselves and the planning of messages within particular cultural contexts. Her research emphasizes how Communication specialists also have a commitment to taking research into the field and engaging in projects from a multidisciplinary perspective.

CONTRIBUTORS

LESLIE A. BAXTER, Ph.D., is F. Wendell Miller Distinguished Professor of Communication Studies at the University of Iowa. Her books, chapters and articles focus on discursive struggle in the meaning-making of families, romantic relationships, and friendships. She is a Distinguished Scholar of the National Communication Association and the first recipient of the WSCA Scholar Award. She has received numerous other awards for her scholarship, including the Brommel Award in family communication, the Miller Book Award in interpersonal communication, and the Knower Article Award in interpersonal communication, all from NCA. She is a former president of WSCA.

PATRICE M. BUZZANELL (Ph.D., Purdue University) is Professor and the W. Charles and Ann Redding Faculty Fellow in the Department of Communication at Purdue University. Her primary interest is in organizational communication, specializing in career, leadership, and work-life issues. She has edited *Rethinking Organizational and Managerial Communication From Feminist Perspectives* (2000), *Gender in Applied Communication Contexts* (2004, with H. Sterk and L. Turner), and *Distinctive Qualities in Communication Research* (2010, with D. Carbaugh). She has published approximately 90 articles and chapters in *Communication Monographs, Human Communication Research, Communication Theory, Human Relations, Journal of Applied Communication Research, Management Communication Quarterly, Handbook of Applied Communication Research, The Sage Handbook on Gender and Communication,* and other journals and handbooks. She has served as editor of *Management Communication Quarterly,* Research Board member for the National Communication Association, and President of the

Organization for the Study of Communication, Language and Gender. Recipient of numerous research, teaching, mentoring, and service awards including NCA's Francine Merritt Award, OSCLG's Teacher-Mentor Award, Purdue's Violet Haas Award, Buzzanell is President of the International Communication Association and President of the Council of Communication Associations. She teaches Purdue's Engineering Projects in Community Service (EPICS) program and currently serves on 13 editorial boards.

JOSEPH N. CAPPELLA, Ph.D., is Professor of Communication and holds the Gerald R. Miller Chair at the Annenberg School for Communication at the University of Pennsylvania. He has been a visiting professor at the University of Pennsylvania and Northwestern University and a visiting scholar at Stanford. His research has focused on health and political communication, social interaction, nonverbal behavior, media effects, and statistical methods and has been supported by grants from NIMH, NIDA, NSF, NCI, NHGRI, The Twentieth Century Fund, and from the Markle, Ford, Carnegie, Pew, and Robert Wood Johnson foundations. He is a Fellow of the International Communication Association and its past president, a distinguished scholar of the National Communication Association, and recipient of the B. Aubrey Fisher Mentorship Award.

DONAL CARBAUGH, (Ph.D., University of Washington) is Professor of Communication, Chair of the International Studies Council (2004–present), and past Co-Chair of the Five College Committee on Native American Indian Studies (2003–2004) at the University of Massachusetts, Amherst. In 2007–2008, he was Fulbright's Distinguished Professor and Bicentennial Chair of North American Studies at the University of Helsinki, Finland. In 1992, he was elected Visiting Senior Member at Linacre College, Oxford University, England, which is a lifetime appointment. He serves as a founding member of a United Nations Institute for Disarmament Research Advisory Group focused on new ways of conducting Security Needs Assessments in "post-conflict societies." His general interests focus upon cultural philosophies of communication, identity, and more specifically, the ways culturally distinctive practices get woven into international and intercultural interactions. He currently serves on more than twenty editorial boards of national and international journals. His published research has appeared in many major academic journals, in several countries including Finland, Germany, Italy, and Russia, in several languages. His most recent book, *Cultures in Conversation*, was designated the Outstanding

Book of the Year by the International and Intercultural Communication Division of the National Communication Association. His first book, *Talking American: Cultural Discourses on DONAHUE*, was identified as "a favorite book of the past 25 years" in *Contemporary Sociology* by former president of the American Sociological Association, William Gamson.

ROBERT T. CRAIG, Ph.D., is a professor in the Department of Communication, University of Colorado at Boulder. His research, which has received awards from both the International Communication Association (ICA) and the National Communication Association (NCA), has addressed a range of topics in communication theory and philosophy, discourse studies, and argumentation with a current focus on the investigation and critical analysis of conceptual assumptions about communication in public discourse. *Theorizing Communication: Readings Across Traditions* (edited with Heidi L. Muller) was published by Sage in 2007. Craig is a member of numerous editorial boards, an advisory editor for the *International Encyclopedia of Communication*, and series editor of the ICA Handbook Series. He is a past president of the International Communication Association (ICA) and was founding editor of the ICA journal, *Communication Theory*.

STANLEY DEETZ, Ph.D., is a President's Teaching Scholar, Professor of Communication and Director of Peace and Conflict Studies at the University of Colorado. His several books focus on corporate governance and communication processes in relation to democracy, micropractices of power and collaborative decision making. He was a Senior Fulbright Scholar and is a National Communication Association Distinguished Scholar and an International Communication Association Past-President and Fellow.

MICHAEL L. HECHT, Ph.D., is a Distinguished Professor of Communication Arts and Sciences at Penn State University. His National Institute on Drug Abuse-funded Drug Resistance Strategies Project was among the first to study the social processes of adolescent drug offers, including an examination of the role of ethnicity and acculturation in these processes, and developed a successful, multicultural, school-based intervention for middle school students. Dr. Hecht has received numerous awards including the National Communication Association's Gerald R. Philips Award for Distinguished Applied Communication Scholarship.

ROBERT C. HORNIK, Ph.D. is the Wilbur Schramm Professor of

Communication and Health Policy at the Annenberg School for Communication, University of Pennsylvania. His major areas of research include health communication, mass media effects and research methods. He has led more than 30 communication campaign evaluations in the U.S. and in 16 other countries, with many focused on AIDS and child survival. He was the scientific director for the evaluation of the U.S. National Youth Anti-Drug Media Campaign and he is currently the director of the University of Pennsylvania's NCI-funded Center of Excellence in Cancer Communication Research. He has received the Mayhew Derryberry Award from the American Public Health Association, the Andreasen Scholar award in social marketing, and the Fisher Mentorship award from the International Communication Association. He most recently edited *Public Health Communication: Evidence for Behavior Change*. Dr. Hornik received a Ph.D. in Communication Research from Stanford University in 1973.

GERRY PHILIPSEN, Ph.D., is Professor of Communication at the University of Washington. His areas of research interest are the ethnography of communication, cultural communication, qualitative field research, and the history of the academic discipline of communication in the twentieth and twenty-first centuries. He is the author of speech codes theory, an empirically-grounded theory of cultural codes of communicative conduct, their nature, their functioning in social interaction, and the ways in which they can be discovered and described. His present work concerns a practical model for guiding individuals' efforts at coming to terms with the cultures of their life worlds. He teaches communication in small groups; communication, conflict, and cooperation; cultural codes in communication; and fieldwork research. At the University of Washington, he has served as department chair, chair of the faculty senate, and secretary of the university faculty.

1

WHAT IS DISTINCTIVE IN COMMUNICATION RESEARCH?

Patrice M. Buzzanell and Donal Carbaugh

The nature of communication research is often a topic of discussion among people who have various interests in it. As individuals who study and live their academic lives, communication researchers periodically ponder what makes their scholarship distinctively *communication* research. In other words, are there qualities that set their research in communication apart from that, for example, in social psychology, linguistics, sociology, anthropology, or psychology? Over the history of communication studies, there have been numerous attempts to define and position the contributions of communication scholars as unique. Some of these identify researchers' interests in the content of and ways in which verbal and nonverbal messages operate. Others sustain interests in varieties of discourse (ranging from micro-practices through macro-societal narratives). Whatever the focus, collections of essays and review articles over the years attest to the difficulty of pinpointing exactly what communication brings to the table in scholarly enterprises as well as in academic life generally.[1] Perhaps the most satisfactory responses to the question are embedded in individual researchers' programs of study, or within particular scholarly traditions.

In order to address the question of what may be distinctive in communication research, we have brought together a range of scholars with exemplary research programs in the study of communication.[2] We have asked each to respond to the question: What characterizes your scholarship as communication research? In other words, how does your type of inquiry treat communication not simply as data, but as its primary theoretical concern? Their responses are the heart of this book.

The resulting edited collection, *Distinctive Qualities in Communication Research*, comes at a particularly opportune time. As in all scholarly fields, ours asks now, and periodically, what is its main subject area, or its contribution to the study of any subject area? In an era of budget cuts and surveys of departments' reputations, deans and administrative leaders sometimes ask what a department of communication offers that is distinctive in its conception and conduct of inquiry. Funding agencies such as the National Science Foundation (NSF), the National Institute of Health (NIH), the Social Science Research Council (SSRC), and so on read proposals and may ask what a communication study contributes to particular social issues and/or funding initiatives that other stances for inquiry may not. A similar exigency is created by a call in many quarters for research teams from multiple disciplines to address a social problem such as AIDS, the removal of dams, environmental assessments, or issues of security and privacy. What does a communication researcher add to such a team? Each such moment provides an opportunity for communication researchers to say what is distinctive about their communication research—its philosophy, theory, methodology, and/or findings.

THE FOLLOWING ESSAYS

Six well-known scholars from the field offer a diverse set of viewpoints on our primary question: Leslie Baxter (University of Iowa), Stan Deetz (University of Colorado Boulder), Michael Hecht (The Pennsylvania State University), Joseph Cappella and Robert Hornik (University of Pennsylvania), and Gerry Philipsen (University of Washington).

In Chapter 2 "A Dialogic Approach to Interpersonal/Family Communication," *Leslie Baxter* describes her position that the unique vantage point of communication lies *not* in understanding communication as mere phenomena nor in the methods for studying it, but in the conceptualization of communication with an emphasis on the "interdependence of messages." Using a dialectical theory of discourses, she illustrates how her approach works to generate insights about teen talk about alcohol use during pregnancy, as well as discourses within step families.

In Chapter 3, *Stan Deetz* discusses "extraordinarily important social problems" about which communication scholars are and should be interested. He advocates an important conceptual shift from topical areas such as identity, power, and institutions, to re-conceptualizations of communication as constitutive of these phenomena, seeing each as an outcome of a communication process itself. His discussion illustrates some of the benefits of treating, for example, power as a dialogic, conversational, and/or discursive practice. Deetz calls his approach a "politically informed social constructionism," and with it he re-locates traditional concerns within communication processes so to help us understand the constitutive power of communication. This process and power, he argues, shape significant features of social life such as the ways decision-making forms relations within and among polities, organizations, and nations.

In Chapter 4, *Michael Hecht* notes several strengths that communication brings to important social problems such as health campaigns, an area in which he has received considerable funding. He understands communication to be "culturally situated message design and interpretation." His focus on cultural communication and indigenous practices generates insights, through participants' stories, into particular groups' sense-making about health, treatment, and message-centered interventions themselves. What has held communication researchers back from funding opportunities, according to Hecht, has been the lack of a grant-getting culture, low aspirations, lack of departmental resources and staff, self-perceptions as teachers and providers of service to campus members (rather than researchers), and the value the Communication field places on journal articles rather than other forms of research. To construct viable remedies for these issues, Hecht argues, communication researchers need to extend their training, understand and conduct large-scale research projects, value applied communication research, and view funded research not only as procuring economic resources but as a way to advance communication research as a means to solving important social problems.

In Chapter 5, *Joseph Cappella and Robert Hornik* focus specifically on communication research as a "practical science," as a rigorous study of "messages and their specific consequences." These authors describe message design with attention to multiple public or target audiences. They discuss particularly how communication research can address the demands in recent funding programs at the National Institute of Health and the National Science Foundation. In the exposition, Cappella and Hornik powerfully demonstrate how a scientific approach to communication achieves theoretical, practical, and social objectives. These are illustrated with current funded projects devoted to health education and cancer research. Although members of the communication discipline may have similar interests to researchers in other fields, the unique aspects of communication inquiries, according to Cappella and Hornik, lie in careful message design as one class of interventions. For instance, the ways in which health care professionals might design actual messages to save lives would be an area in which the field has an important tradition and one that encourages funding agencies to support a communication scholar within a multidisciplinary team.

In Chapter 6, *Gerry Philipsen* proposes that some communication researchers might think too small, and may benefit, indeed, from linking their thinking about communication to cultural features and forms. He encourages scholars to figure out how to work with others from different disciplines and from various cultural communities in mutually productive ways. He demonstrates how a network of ethnographers of communication is doing just that. In his own research, he has not only analyzed but engaged in the discourses of different disciplines. For example, he worked with a physical scientist to unveil better ways of speaking in elementary science classes. He reviews similar accomplishments of other ethnographic works in settings of health, in groups of immigrant peoples, in nanotechnology laboratories, and in various communities around the world through a Security Needs Assessment Project. Through this type of ethnographic inquiry, he surveys how this network of scholars has developed theories for understanding communication as a cultural and interactional phenomenon. For Philipsen, a central problem that communication researchers sometimes confront in a community of non-communication scholars is a lack of traction, so to speak, in talking about Communication itself as a discipline of thought. In this sense, there is sometimes a productive tension between the disciplinarity of Communication and the ways other scholars understand it as a subject matter, and the relation of that to their perspective on difficult social problems. His chapter shows a broad range of theoretical and practical applications of a communication view to such difficult problems.

A CAVEAT AND MORE

We readily admit that there are only five distinguished scholars whose views are represented prominently in this volume. If we had approached the content of this book differently, we might have divided the chapters according to (a) contexts; (b) meta-theoretical traditions; (c) communication dimensions; (d) dialectics of theory-practice and/or scholarship-activism; and (e) agency-voice dynamics. We conclude this section with (f) specific caveats and other possibilities that suggest alternative organizing logics for our book.

First, we could have organized contextually, that is, through interpersonal, intercultural, organizational, mass, or other situations of communication. However, as these scholars show us, it is only through crossing contexts and examining the processes that converge and diverge around central questions about how communication is formative of any given setting that we come to specific conceptualizations about the nature of communication. It is a focus on these and their distinctiveness which provides the central theme of this book.

Of course, we can look to earlier schemes for depicting our field. Second, we could use Robert Craig's (1999) meta-theoretical framework. Using this, Craig's taxonomy, we could have included rhetoric (and the arts of suasory expression), semiotics (the study of signs, symbols, their reference and the relationships and the webs of meaning that get built through sign systems), phenomenology (the study of people's lived experience in the world, the nature of consciousness and conscious engagement in the world), cybernetics (the study of systems or overlapping, nested systems of interrelated elements that are interdependent with one another), social psychology (the study of social, and societal bases of identities and relationships), a socio-cultural studies scholar (the study of distinctive processes of meaning-making and the critical reflection on those means), and a critical theorist (the systematic critique of dis/empowering presuppositions). As we reflect upon Craig's framework, however, we think the scholars whose works are included in this volume touch a bit on each of these. We have, across the research programs examined here, instances of ethno-rhetoric, interpretations of symbols and symbolic expression, information as captured and designed in messages, issues of social identity and interpersonal relations, a variety of cultural and critical studies. We could give more detailed accounting of each, but simply mention them here as a way of introducing a range of intellectual concerns and traditions. As a result, perhaps none of our contributors fits solely within one of these (i.e., Craig's) traditions, rather than the others. Of course, traditional placement was not Craig's intent. Rather, he had hoped to identify dimensions of scholarship that could enhance discussion of our field, its theories, and concerns. And it is in that spirit of engaged discussion, that we mention his seven traditions here.

Third, we also could use Deetz's (1996) dimensions of communication similarly, noting that we have representatives from each discourse, all the while admitting that scholarship does not fit easily within any single "quadrant", (see Figure 1.1). We could note that Deetz aligns his critical–political view with the dissensus aspects of our field; Leslie Baxter operates within a dialogic view, while Gerry Philipsen integrates normative and interpretive modes, giving voice to individuals' ways of

Dissensus

Dialogic studies, postmodern, deconstructionist	Critical Studies, late modern, reformist
Interpretive studies, premodern, traditional	Normative studies, modern, progressive

Local ← → A priori

Consensus

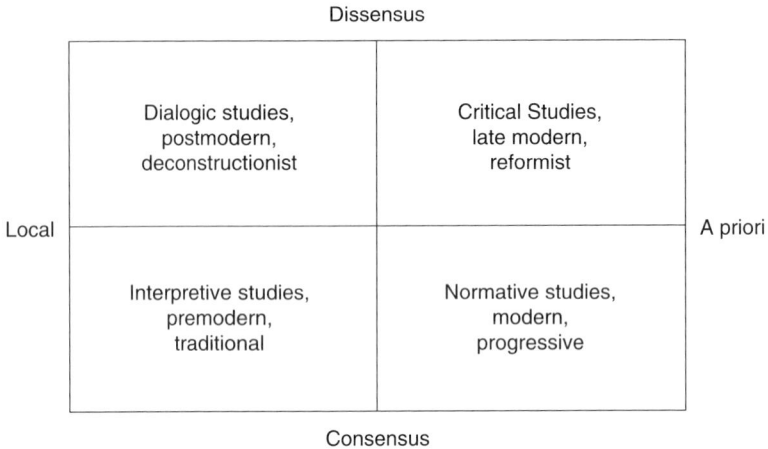

Figure 1.1 Adapted from Deetz's (1996) discursive spaces embodying social resources for research.

speaking about their situations. Michael Hecht is, in his way, normative with critical interventions in view, while Joe Cappella and Robert Hornik adopt, primarily, a more normative and progressive stance. All of these forms of scholarly inquiry help our field construct and maintain a range of rich and diverse insights into social issues, demonstrating our field's unique ability to emphasize process, particularly communication processes as central to the conduct of social and cultural lives. The range of approaches also demonstrates a complementary set of methodologies to the study of communication. In each quadrant and across quadrants, we see different ways of creating knowledge claims, building theory, and establishing judgments. Treating the group of approaches in this way—focused on dimensions of consensus and dissensus, comparative methodologies, knowledge claims—brings discussion of them, as with Craig's template, to a metatheoretical level, reflecting upon how theories are constituted, what commitments are being made through each, what methodological implications emerge, and how important practical outcomes contribute to local interests as well as the larger society. The range of social problems being addressed is indeed impressive in what follows throughout this edited collection, from alcohol use and pregnancy, to step-families, to large-scale health campaigns, to power relations, to cancer treatments, and to nanotechnology and issues of national and local security.

Furthermore, the discussion also indicates stances toward traditional dialectics of theory-practice and scholarship-activism—meaning that research not only provides insight about society as communicative processes, but also suggests possible directions for various types of pragmatic actions. In the following chapters, each scholar describes specific directions of application based upon the assumptions she or he makes. Each responds with concrete examples to the charge that communication research should have a social impact, can set an agenda for social change all the while embracing a range in their involvement, stances toward human participants, and the social phenomena at hand.

Fifth, we also note a range of stances toward agency and voice in the five chapters in this collection. For Leslie Baxter, Gerry Philipsen, and Stan Deetz, agency functions at interactional levels where one conversational turn or textual phase or organizational formation is implicated in another, then another, and so on. Similarly, voice operates at very personal or individual interactional levels for Baxter, at a mid- or abstract-range for Cappella and Hornick, and yet also at more political and cultural levels for Deetz, Hecht, and Philipsen. These of course are not mutually exclusive concerns, as each voice is distinct from yet can complement the others.

Finally, missing from our collection are of course many outstanding researchers and perspectives. Given a small volume, the omissions were by necessity. Our goals were not to offer a comprehensive account of all the different theories and distinctions in our field, nor to provide a comprehensive overview of a particular researcher's work. Instead, we asked our contributors to focus on the single question of distinctive qualities in their work, as *communication* research, using their own program of studies as examples. In doing so, we have asked our contributors to stake out a position and to argue for the distinctively communicational aspects of their approach.

All chapter authors in our book take, as an imperative and a given, the worth of studying actual messages or ways of speaking or discourses, and do so with the belief that doing this type of research will reveal something important about human communicative capabilities and its shaping of lives. We do not include many other important programs of work in, for example, conversation analysis, rhetoric, journalism, and new media technologies or mass communication. We also have not included postcolonial and subaltern communication research that endeavors to critique ideological configurations of the Western world and their concomitant practices and that, in their own way, give voice to marginalized group members. While some studies in Hecht's, Deetz's and Philipsen's programs of work accomplish these ends, there are more approaches and other researchers that could and perhaps should be included.

Similarly, we have included neither network analysis nor specific versions of feminist scholarship. Feminist communication studies may be different from the linguistic or performance turns that occur in other disciplines because of feminist communication researchers' emphases on praxis, the power of communication in constituting particular phenomena, and an engagement with groups of people considered vulnerable and underserved in specific socio-cultural–economic–political locations. Some of these concerns are addressed by the approaches advocated by our contributors.

Importantly, these chapters present the authors' struggle with the tensions in our field. As their own research has evolved, they have needed to contend with theory-practice questions, challenges from alternative theories, paradigmatic movements and desires for consistency, and findings that make no sense when explanatory tools that are known at that time are used. They illustrate the notion that what we think about the nature of the world, how people engage with the world, and how individuals and communities construct knowledge—even what constitutes knowledge and truth(s)—have profound implications for the nature of communication work and how we present our discipline to ourselves and others. In fact, these processes—thoughtful engagement, knowledge, and truth—may be properly considered as the very nature and outcomes of communication practice itself.

As noted at the outset of this section, there are other ways to categorize the scholarship in our field. These different ways, as the chapters that follow, depict multivocality in our field, meaning that there is as enormous a range of perspectives in the field, as there are in others. There's a great deal of ferment, a great deal of disagreement about a wide variety of things. To respond adequately to this ferment, scholars have organized our discipline in varied ways. Not only is the question about how we organize differences essential but we also must live with these differences—that is, the ways in which we conceptualize and organize our views of communication itself.[3]

SPECIAL FEATURES OF THE BOOK

The following collection is of five chapters which are outlined above. In addition, we strive to create a dialogue about the issues the book raises and addresses. As a result, we've designed our book to have a few special features.

First, we open with both a Foreword from a well-known scholar of communication, Bob Craig, who introduces his thoughts on the volume. Also, we open with this introduction from the co-editors that provides a preview of the specific purposes and content of the volume as well as alternative ways of engaging with chapter materials and broader conceptualizations of our field.

A second feature of the book is a special suggested readings for each chapter. We have requested that each author supply a suggested reading list that provides instructors and students with central, supplementary materials for each chapter. The lists could be consulted for further study about the distinctive qualities under discussion in each chapter. Following the organization of an earlier book on "watershed research traditions in human communication" (Cushman & Kovacic, 1995), we requested that each reading list include four parts, or four types of readings. One set of references leads readers to the philosophical foundations of the approach; a second set includes further readings in the theory, or central concepts, being explicated or presumed in the chapter; a third set offers elaborations on the methodology in use when doing the research the chapter discusses; and a fourth includes citations to specific case studies, or applications of the approach under discussion. The point of each reading list is NOT the creation of a comprehensive bibliography on the approach; it is to give readers references to the best sources for further understanding the philosophy, theory, methodology, and case studies using the approach. In other words, the reading lists consist of a few "best works" for each of the four parts, rather than all possible work done from that approach.

More specifically, these following readings, and the special references, enable readers to delve into fundamental questions in our field and disciplines. Through the chapters and supplementary materials, readers can examine epistemology or the question of how one can know communication. They also can seek further to understand more fully the ontology of an approach, or the nature of being presumed as a communicant; what is the nature of the phenomenon in the world? What is our manner of engagement with this world? And most basic, what is the nature of the world itself? Each approach explicitly claims, or implies something about praxis, the practical art of action and argument, and also something about phronesis, value-laden action and judgment. What does scholarship about communicative action and judgment mean to society? How does it or does it not have value in society? Every theory makes important claims about what society is, what it should be, how humans can live together and manage society to make it better achieve its capabilities. The chapters offer responses to these questions; the supplemental reading lists offer further insights.

Finally, we close with our final chapter. Although not a "special feature" *per se*, this chapter summarizes five qualities, across the chapters, which we identify as distinctive in the communication research assembled here. We leave the reader with these remarks, but also by extending the invitation to engage, challenge or revise, the question: What is distinctive in communication research?

NOTES

1. One of the landmark definitional endeavors in the social sciences is Jesse Delia's (1987) overview. Since that time, other discussions have appeared in handbooks, edited collections, and journals, such as the Chautauqua series of invited essays in *Communication Monographs* under the editorship of Judee Burgoon (e.g., Brant Burleson, 1992). Similar theoretical overviews have stressed how a few research traditions in Communication have produced distinctive philosophical commitments, theoretical frameworks, and insightful findings (e.g., Cushman & Kovacic, 1995). More recently, Bob Craig's (1999) article on the metatheoretical discourses in the field of communication aims to put the various epistemological and ontological orientations in conversation with each other to dispel claims of such profound incommensurability that scholars from one part of the field cannot converse with others. In addition, various textbooks have utilized Craig's framework to organize their discussions, most notably Stephen Littlejohn and Karen Foss (2008), and Bob Craig and Heidi Muller (2007). Different organizational patterns cover epistemological, ontological, and other foundational assumptions for communication and can be found in books and edited collections, such as those by James Anderson (1996), and Greg Shepherd, Jeff St. John, and Ted Striphas (2006).
2. By "exemplary," we mean each scholar has produced what Cushman and Kovacic (1995) have identified as a "watershed research tradition," that is, a collaborative program of work which meets four criteria: a deep philosophy, an explicit theoretical stance, a detailed methodology, and focused applications.
3. One historical way of organizing the differences in theories is based on the idea that context drives important differences in findings and applications (with context ranging from dyadic, to group, organizational, national, and international). Another is proposed by Putnam and others (e.g., Putnam, Phillips, & Chapman, 1996; Putnam & Boys, 2006; Coopman, 2003) who envision communication as a series of metaphorical schema that illuminate how, why, and for what consequences communication operates in different contexts. These metaphors include communication as linkage, conduit, performance, discourse, voice, and contradiction.

   Similarly, other scholars have proposed using "problematics," namely, the central intellectual concerns that occur within our discipline and as "stances on theory" whereby communication researchers delve into the deeply held assumptions and choices that guide particular research programs (Shepherd et al., 2006). With regard to problematics, Mumby and Stohl

(1996, 2007; see also Broadfoot & Munshi, 2007a, 2007b; Kirby, Golden, Medved, Jorgenson, & Buzzanell, 2003) describe four that are particularly important to the organizational context (i.e., voice, rationality, organization, and organization-society). Shepherd et al.'s (2006) stances are organized around processes of making, materializing, contextualizing, politicizing, and questioning theory.

Other categorization schemes focus less on context, metaphors, organizing logics, central problematics, and stances than on paradigmatic lenses for communication research. In that regard, literature could be characterized as functionalist, interpretive, or critical-postmodern (Craig, 1999), or as discourses of representation, understanding, suspicion, and vulnerability (see Mumby, 1997) with associated sets of assumptions, research questions, and methodologies for each. As much as we have tried to open up this conversation to alternative schemes, we have, of necessity, limited the variety of metatheoretical moments and insights that have laid out different schemes for understanding the field of communication.

REFERENCES

Anderson, J. A. (1996). *Communication theory: Epistemological foundations.* New York: Guilford.

Broadfoot, K. J., & Munshi, D. (2007a). Diverse voices and alternative rationalities: Imagining forms of postcolonial organizational communication. *Management Communication Quarterly, 21,* 249–267.

Broadfoot, K. J., & Munshi, D. (2007b). Afterword: In search of a polyphony of voices. *Management Communication Quarterly, 21,* 281–283.

Burleson, B. R. (1992). Taking communication seriously. *Communication Monographs, 59,* 79–86.

Coopman, S. J. (2003). Communicating disability: Metaphors of oppression, metaphors of empowerment. In P. Kalbfleisch (Ed.), *Communication yearbook 27* (pp. 337–394). Mahwah, NJ: LEA.

Craig, R. T. (1999). Communication theory as a field. *Communication Theory, 9,* 119–161.

Craig, R. T., & Muller, H. L. (Eds.). (2007). *Theorizing communication: Readings across traditions.* Thousand Oaks, CA: Sage.

Cushman, D. & Kovacic, B. (Eds.). (1995). *Watershed research traditions in human communication theory.* Albany, NY: State University of New York Press.

Deetz, S. (1996). Describing differences in approaches to organization science: Rethinking Burrell and Morgan and their legacy. *Organization Science, 7,* 191–207.

Delia, J. G. (1987). Communication research: A history. In C. R. Berger, & S. H. Chaffee (Eds.), *Handbook of communication science* (pp. 20–98). Newbury Park, CA: Sage.

Kirby, E., Golden, A., Medved, C., Jorgenson, J., & Buzzanell, P. M. (2003). An organizational communication challenge to the discourse of work and family research: From problematics to empowerment. In P. Kalbfleisch (Ed.), *Communication yearbook 27* (pp. 1–44). Mahwah, NJ: Lawrence Erlbaum Associates, Inc.

Littlejohn, S. W., & Foss, K. A. (2008). *Theories of human communication* (9th ed). Belmont, CA: Thomson Learning/Wadsworth.

Mumby, D. K. (1997). Modernism, postmodernism, and communication studies: A rereading of an ongoing debate. *Communication Theory, 7,* 1–28.

Mumby, D. K., & Stohl, C. (1996). Disciplining organizational communication studies. *Management Communication Quarterly, 10,* 50–72.

Mumby, D. K., & Stohl, C. (2007). (Re)disciplining organizational communication studies: A response to Broadfoot and Munshi. *Management Communication Quarterly, 21,* 268–280.

Putnam, L. L., & Boys, S. (2006). Revisiting metaphors of organizational communication. In S. R. Clegg (Ed.), *Handbook of organization studies* (pp. 541–576). Thousand Oaks, CA: Sage.

Putnam, L. L., Phillips, N., & Chapman, P. (1996). Metaphors of communication and organization. In S. R. Clegg, C. Hardy, & W. Nord (Eds.), *Handbook of organization studies* (pp. 375–408). London: Sage.

Shepherd, G., St. John, J., & Striphas, T. (2006). *Communication as . . .: Perspectives on theory.* Thousand Oaks, CA: Sage.

2

A DIALOGIC APPROACH TO INTERPERSONAL/ FAMILY COMMUNICATION

Leslie A. Baxter

My favorite theorist, the 1930s Russian scholar of culture and language, Mikhail Bakhtin, put it this way:

> In what way will the event be enriched if I succeed in fusing with the other? If instead of two, there is now just one? What do I gain by having the other fuse with me? Let him rather stay on the outside because from there he can know and see what I cannot see or know from my vantage point, and can thus enrich essentially the event of my life. (quoted in Todorov, 1984, p. 108)

Said differently, it does no good simply to mirror Other; we need to have a unique vantage point. In the context of this book, the ability of Communication Studies to contribute to the interdisciplinary conversation is contingent on our collective ability to give voice to perspectives not yet heard. The context for my remarks is interpersonal/ family communication, the area with which I am most familiar. I will first discuss more broadly the possible bases upon which a claim to distinctiveness can be made, then I will launch into a discussion of my own research program in developing and applying relational dialectics theory (Baxter & Montgomery, 1996) to the study of relationship challenges, particularly in the context of families.

POSSIBLE BASES OF DISTINCTIVENESS

It seems to me that there are only four possible ways for Communication Studies to claim itself as intellectually distinct from other fields of study:

1. Uniqueness in the study of communication as a phenomenon in its own right.
2. Uniqueness in how we study communication phenomena, i.e., methods.
3. Uniqueness in how we conceptualize communication phenomena.
4. Uniqueness in how we theorize communication phenomena.

I will briefly share my observations for each of these domains of potential distinctiveness.

Uniqueness in Our Focus Communication as an Object of Study

Many scholars in other disciplines hold interpersonal/family communication phenomena as their object of study. This results in a Janus-like effect. At its worst, it suggests to deans and others that communication scholars are no different from everybody else who studies interpersonal/family communication, thus obviating the need to legitimate us as a discrete field, with its own bureaucratic foothold in the academic race for space, budgetary dollars, and new faculty lines. I am frankly discouraged when I still pick up recent handbooks and other edited volumes presumably devoted to interpersonal/family communication and observe that the majority of contributing authors and cited literature comes from other disciplines, most notably Psychology and Sociology. I don't want to appear xenophobic in my concern about the pervasiveness of "outside" scholars who study interpersonal/family communication. Indeed, their contributions are exceedingly valuable. But we risk being reduced to a mere intellectual site—a holding bin—for others to dominate the study of interpersonal/family communication phenomena unless we can somehow demonstrate that we study communication in ways that are unique from that afforded by, say, a psychological footing. In sum, I don't find much of a foothold for distinctiveness in this first possible claim.

Uniqueness in the Methods Used to Study Interpersonal/Family Communication Phenomena

I also don't think this is the foundation upon which to build the claim of distinctiveness. The toolkit used by interpersonal/family communication scholars has the same six methods as other social scientific endeavors (Baxter & Babbie, 2004): for quantitatively oriented researchers, the triad of the experiment, the survey, and quantitative text analysis; for qualitatively oriented researchers, the triad of participant-observation, unstructured interviewing, and qualitative text analysis. So, let's turn to the next possible basis of distinctiveness, where I think we begin to see some intellectual traction.

Uniqueness in How Interpersonal/Family Communication is Conceptualized

I think it's fair to say that most laypersons, including scholars in disciplines outside of Communication Studies, view communication as a transmission activity (Penman, 2000). That is, communication is viewed as a conduit technology for transmitting representations of an external world or a speaker's internal mind. In fact, the majority of interpersonal/family communication researchers are still located in the representational project and thus function to reproduce it. The transmission project is centered in a technical approach organized around getting messages across better, improving understanding, and so forth.

But an alternative view has emerged in the study of interpersonal/family communication. Depending on who you are and your paradigmatic inclinations, this alternative goes by various labels and takes several forms, but collectively this alternative view articulates a focus on communication as an *interactive process of meaning-making*: an emergent process that happens not in isolated individuals who produce and consume stand-alone messages but instead in the *interdependence of messages*. This conceptualization is a view that I think we can uniquely bring to the interdisciplinary table.

Bakhtin labels this alternative conceptualization as the "chain of speech communion" (1986, p. 93). Central to the speech-communion chain is the recognition that a given utterance is always already a response to some prior utterance and that it is always directed toward an anticipated utterance-response. Bakhtin's dialogic perspective has been central to my research program for the past decade and a half, and I present a portion of it as one way to highlight communication as an interactive, interdependent process.

Utterances are sites where a variety of kinds of discourses, or systems of meaning, are at play. Four in particular merit discussion (Baxter & Montgomery, 1996). First, some of the links in the speech-communion chain are quite distant in space and time; these distal links represent the already-spoken utterances of the past that occurred prior to a particular encounter, and I will refer to them as *distal already-spokens*.

Whenever we speak, argued Bakhtin, we use words that are already populated with others' prior utterances or with our own utterances from the past. For example, a distal dialogic overtone can often be found in a couple's idiomatic expressions in which they invoke some important relationship event from their history together (e.g., Baxter, 1987, 1992; Baxter & Pittman, 2001). In addition, utterances in the here-and-now "speak culture" are riddled throughout with any number of already circulating social/cultural ideologies. It is difficult, for example, to hear relationship parties talk to each other, or to talk about their relationship to a researcher, without giving voice to discourses of individualism, romantic love, and privacy that circulate in the broader social milieu of U.S. society. The study of socio/cultural distal voices in parties' relational communication has occupied much of my research effort, and I will return to a discussion of some of these findings in the next section of the chapter.

Second, other utterances in the chain of speech communion are more proximal; for example, other utterances in the parties' conversation at hand. These discursive links represent dialogic overtones with the already-spokens of the current interaction event, and I will refer to them as *proximal already-spokens*. Rituals are important interaction events, well documented as important to relational and family well-being (for a review, see Baxter & Braithwaite, 2006), and nicely illustrate the concept of proximal already-spokens. Several scholars have argued that rituals are meaningful because they work at many layers of meaning at once, and thereby hold opposing or competing discourses (Baxter & Braithwaite, 2006). For example, Dawn Braithwaite and I have examined the ritual of marriage renewal vows, finding that it celebrates marriage as both a private and a public relationship, as a site of both stability and change, and as both a conventionalized institution and a uniquely crafted culture of two (Braithwaite & Baxter, 1995). From a socio/cultural perspective, it performs the competing ideologies of individualism and community (Baxter & Braithwaite, 2002).

The third and fourth kinds of discourse shift attention from the past to the anticipated future. Utterances not only reverberate with dialogic voices of already-spokens; in addition, they are laced with the dialogic overtones of utterances that are anticipated to follow. Similar to the proximal and distant voices of the already-spokens, proximal and distant voices can be identified with the not-yet-spokens in the chain of speech communion. An utterance takes into account the immediate addressee's possible responses—the *proximal not-yet-spokens*, the third kind of discourse. As Bakhtin (1986, p. 95) observed, "An essential (constitutive) marker of the utterance is its quality of being directed to someone, its addressivity." For example, many stepchildren report a hesitation to disclose to the resident parent their frustrations with the stepparent based on the anticipation that the parent has developed a coalition with the new spouse and will respond negatively (Baxter, Braithwaite, & Bryant, 2006).

Fourth, and last, an addressee can be distant, as well; others who are not a fellow participant-interlocutor in the immediate conversation but who may respond to the utterance at some future point. I will refer to this as the *distal not-yet spokens*. For example, in the stepfamily context, many parents report that they prefer written e-mail exchanges with the ex-spouse instead of oral exchanges in anticipation of being able to show them to a judge if it becomes necessary to renegotiate the custody arrangements stipulated in the divorce decree (Schrodt, Baxter, McBride, Braithwaite, & Fine, 2006). In this instance, the judge is functioning as an anticipated addressee who is absent at the time of the e-mail exchange between the divorced parents. The anticipated addressee could be a specific person, as in the case of the judge, or the generalized other of Bakhtin's (1986) superaddressee. The super-addressee is akin to "people in general" or "society," and invokes communicators' conception of what is regarded as normative or ideal. For example, many stepchildren often refer to their stepfamily in negative ways, for example, "He's not my real dad" or "We're not a real family" (Baxter, Braithwaite, Bryant, & Wagner, 2004). These stepchildren have internalized a discourse that positions the nuclear, biological family as the ideal, giving voice to others' criticisms of them as somehow not "real."

In short, dialogism's utterance is far from an isolated act of a sovereign individual. It isn't even a duet between two speakers. It is more like an ensemble in which the simultaneous interplay of multiple, different discourses—distant and proximal, already-spoken and not-yet-spoken—produce meaning at the moment (Baxter, 2004). This intertextuality of discourses exemplifies the interdependence of messages that I think is an important element of our claim to conceptual distinctiveness.

A Bakhtinian approach to communication empowers communication to create or construct the social world, including self, other, and the relationship between them. Logically, if meaning emerges out of interdependence of messages, then it cannot be a closed system and, of necessity, becomes unfinalizable (Bakhtin, 1981, 1990). By contrast, the transmission view of communication emphasizes a reproductive function of communication. Reproduction presumes a social world already given, whereas a dialogic approach asks how communication creates social reality (Baxter, 2007). As Bakhtin (1986, pp. 118–119) indicated, "An utterance is never just a reflection or an expression of something already existing outside it that is given and final." In short, an alternative committed to the interdependence of messages opens up the possibility for what many are describing as a social constructionist, or constitutive, approach to communication (see Craig, 1999). However, there are many social constructionist approaches to communication. The unique contribution of Bakhtin's dialogic project is an articulation of the generative mechanism for the constitutive, meaning-making process: the interplay of different discourses (Baxter, 2007).

The power of communication to create begins with consciousness, in what amounts to a de-centering of the sovereign self. Bakhtin's (1984) fragmented notes for his intended revision of *Problems of Dostoevsky's Poetics* made the argument that there is nothing sovereign, or autonomous, about the self:

> The most important acts constituting self-consciousness are determined by a relationship toward another consciousness. Separation, dissociation, and enclosure within the self as the main reason for the loss of one's self. Not that which takes place within, but that which takes place on the boundary between one's own and someone else's consciousness, on the threshold . . . To be means to communicate . . . A person has no sovereign territory, he is wholly and always on the boundary. (p. 287)

In de-centering the sovereign self, the Bakhtin project moves interpersonal/family communication away from its psychological moorings in cognitive science, shifting us instead to discursive intertextuality. Individual consciousness is re-conceptualized as the interplay of different discourses; thinking is thus re-conceived as a discursive exercise. An individual's utterance is less an index to his or her mind and more a site of multiple discourses at play.

De-centering the sovereign self opens up new questions for scholarly research that stand in contrast to more psychologically-based work. As I have elsewhere argued (Baxter, 2004; Baxter & Montgomery, 1996), much of this work views the self as a pre-formed identity prior to entry into relationships. Self-disclosure, one of the most frequently studied variables of the past three decades, is viewed as the key communicative device through which this pre-formed self is made known to another in establishing and maintaining relationships (e.g., Altman & Taylor, 1973). In de-centering the sovereign self, the question becomes how self, and relatedly social identity, are ongoingly formed through relating.

The conception of the self as pre-formed is an important ingredient in the American ideologies of individualism (e.g., Bellah, Madsen, Sullivan, Swidler, & Tipton, 1985) and romantic love (e.g., Bachen & Illouz, 1996). For example, as I have argued elsewhere (Baxter & Akkoor, 2006), the ideology of romantic love is organized around a logic of individualistic self-interest. A person "falls in love" with another because of an attraction to him or her based on reward potential. The attraction–love association that prevails in the ideology of romantic love evidences what Bellah and colleagues referred to as the therapeutic ideal of love: "The therapeutic attitude reinforces the traditional individualism of American culture, including the concept of utilitarian individuals maximizing their own interests" (1985, p. 104). For those enthralled with the therapeutic attitude, "obligation of any kind becomes problematic in relationships" (Bellah et al., 1985, p. 101). Clearly, this view of love supports a view of marriage as a disposable institution. It also positions us to adopt the ethnocentric view that other conceptions of love and marriage are inferior. For example, arranged marriages, which are still quite prevalent in non-Western societies, are "looked on with pity or even moral condemnation" (Moore, 1998, p. 264) by scholars and laypersons alike because they are not grounded in the ideology of romantic love. This derogation persists in spite of substantial research suggesting that arranged marriages overall are stable, long-lasting, based on long-term commitment, and satisfying to the partners (e.g., Myers, Madathil, & Tingle, 2005).

To argue that dialogic communication empowers communication to be creative is not to claim that interlocutors never engage in reproductive activity. In fact, utterances often are characterized by authoritative voices in which a single point of view is privileged and others are relatively muted. Bakhtin argued that intertextuality is rarely a level playing field: "Every concrete utterance of a speaking subject serves as a point where centrifugal as well as centripetal forces are brought to bear" (1981, p. 272). Competing discourses, some more marginalized than others, jockey to emerge as the centripetal center of meaning in the process of intertextual struggle. I will elaborate on this struggle of competing discourses below.

I do not want to imply that the dialogic project is the only way to deliver the intellectual goods on interactivity and interdependence of messages; far from it. But it is one way, and the way I have personally found fruitful. In conceptualizing communication as the interdependence of messages, we have a source of traction in our claim to distinctiveness. Let me turn to the fourth possible basis for a claim of distinctiveness, where we gain further intellectual traction.

Uniqueness in How Communication Phenomena are Theorized

Since conceptualization and theory are close cousins, I have already been sharing with you elements of my own Relational Dialectics Theory (RDT), which is nothing more than a dialogic approach to relationship communication (Baxter, 2004, 2006; Baxter & Braithwaite, in press b; Baxter & Montgomery, 1996). I am pleased to observe that home-grown theories of interpersonal and family communication are blossoming, and that RDT is but one seedling in the intellectual nursery of interpersonal/family communication!

The backdrop for this claim is a pair of essays authored by Charles Berger. His classic 1991 essay in *Communication Monographs* noted the paucity of home-grown communication theories and our resultant import–export problem; that is, our reliance on theories developed by others in other disciplines. By contrast, his 2005 essay in the *Journal of Communication* identified sufficient progress, with enough home-grown communication theories to afford a review essay devoted to them! Dawn Braithwaite and I, as part of two book projects, one on family communication theory (Braithwaite & Baxter, 2006) and the other on interpersonal communication theory (Baxter & Braithwaite, in press b), have recently completed content analyses of the data-based research published in communication journals in these two domains from 1990 to now. Our findings mirror the shift noted by Berger. With respect to family communication, we identified close to 300 data-based research articles, finding that 43% of them displayed theoretical presence of some kind—either *a priori* or post hoc use of an existing theory to render findings predictable or intelligible or efforts to inductively develop theory. I am pleased that almost half of the top 20 most frequently cited theories in the family communication literature are home-grown efforts by scholars from Communication Studies. As for interpersonal communication, we identified close to 1000 data-based research studies, of which about two-thirds evidenced theoretical presence of some kind. Our in-press volume that reviews the dominant theories in interpersonal communication evidences that over half of the theories are home-grown by Communication Studies scholars. To me, these findings document the tremendous growth that has taken place over the past decade and a half in efforts to develop our own theories. This strengthens tremendously our ability to make unique contributions to the interdisciplinary conversation, as we shift from being the proverbial handmaiden who services other disciplines' theories to assume an independent disciplinary voice.

With the humble recognition that my work with RDT is but one home-grown theory among a growing number, let me turn to a discussion of it in order to fulfill the editors' charge that authors elaborate on how their approach to research has contributed insights to our understanding of communication in addressing social issues or problems.

RELATIONAL DIALECTICS THEORY, APPLIED

RDT is an interpretive theory of meaning-making in familial and interpersonal relationships. However, unlike many interpretive theories, RDT challenges interpretivism's focus on consensual, unified meanings and emphasizes instead the fragmented and contested nature of meaning-making. Further, the theory shifts from a focus on individual subjective sense-making to a focus on utterances. The theory is most amenable to qualitative methods, although quantitatively-oriented work has also been conducted using the theory.

The core proposition of RDT is that meanings emerge from the struggle of different, often opposing, ideologically-freighted discourses. RDT is skeptical of what Bakhtin called authoritative discourses (Bakhtin, 1981, 1984)—dominant meanings that become calcified as the normative, taken-for-granted meanings. Instead, RDT emphasizes the struggle of competing discourses. To date, colleagues and I have explored the competing discourses that animate a variety of relationships, including: co-workers in organizational settings (e.g., Baxter, 1993; Bridge & Baxter, 1992); romantic and marital pairs (e.g., Baxter, 1990; Baxter & Braithwaite, 2002; Baxter, Braithwaite, Golish, & Olson, 2002; Baxter & Erbert, 1999; Baxter & Simon, 1993; Baxter & Widenmann, 1993; Braithwaite & Baxter, 1995; Sahlstein & Baxter, 2001); platonic friendships (e.g., Baxter, Foley, & Thatcher, 2006; Baxter et al., 1997; Baxter & West, 2003); and stepfamilies (see below).

Three discursive struggles are commonly articulated across different relationship types, because they draw upon broader socio/cultural discourses that circulate in American society. Relationship parties often give voice to a discourse of autonomy that interpenetrates with a discourse of connection, reflecting basic American cultural ideologies of individualism and community, respectively (Bellah et al., 1985). Parties also give voice to a discourse of openness, candor, and honesty, a pervasive cultural motif in dominant American society, which struggles with a competing discourse of discretion rooted in a broader cultural ideology that supports the right to privacy. Third, relationship talk can be heard as a discursive struggle of tradition and conventionality with and against a discourse that values uniqueness and change. These "big 3" discursive struggles take particularistic form from one relationship type to another.

The practical import of the RDT emphasis on competing discourses is three-fold. First, the complexity of dialectical struggles forecloses overly facile social prescriptions that are pervasive on self-help bookstore shelves, such as "always be open" or "always put your partner's needs ahead of your own." Such one-sided prescriptions function to silence the competing discourses that cannot reasonably be ignored; for example, discourses of privacy and individualism. Second, RDT argues that discursive struggles are inherent in relating, not a warning signal that a relationship is "in trouble." This second implications helps us to reclaim conflict as positive for relationship parties. Third, RDT underscores the unfinalizability of relating. Discursive struggles are ongoing for relationship parties, and new meanings have the potential to emerge in every interaction event. Relationships can never reach a point of fixed closure, and perceptions to the contrary are naïve at best.

However, RDT is committed to a local, particularistic understanding of how competing discourses animate specific relational experiences, not merely to the general value of attending to discursive struggles or to a search for abstract commonalities that gain widespread articulation across relationship types. In the interests of illustrating how RDT can help us understand the role of communication in addressing social problems, I am going to discuss two different applications in the domain of family communication that colleagues and I have made of RDT. The first is a funded project designed to increase understanding among lower-income, rural, pregnant women of the dangers of alcohol consumption during pregnancy and to marshal the support of the social network in talking about these dangers with pregnant women. The second is a series of studies focused on a rapidly growing, yet problematic, family form—the stepfamily.

Discursive Struggles in Talk about Alcohol Use during Pregnancy

The major health risk to infants whose mothers drank during pregnancy is fetal alcohol syndrome (FAS), the leading known preventable cause of mental retardation (National Institute on Alcohol Abuse and Alcoholism [NIAAA], 2000b). In the decades since FAS was discovered, more than 1,000 research articles have been published on the topic (NIAAA, 2000a); however, prevention has received only limited attention. Because FAS is preventable through behavioral change, colleagues and I undertook a project funded by the Department of Health and Human Services, Public Health Service, and Centers for Disease Control to develop and implement a community-based media campaign targeted at lower-income, rural Iowa women and designed to change their communication practices related to decision-making about drinking alcohol during pregnancy. In the formative phase of the project, we conducted qualitative interviews with a sample of women from the target population (Baxter, Hirokawa, Lowe, Pearce, & Nathan, 2004). Findings revealed the importance of the social network in the decision to drink, especially the role of other female friends and family members. Further, two competing socio/cultural ideologies were identified that animated decision-making surrounding the legitimacy of talking about alcohol use during pregnancy: the discourse of individualism and the discourse of responsible motherhood. These two competing discourses show remarkable resemblance to Hays' (1996) articulation of two cultural ideologies of motherhood in contemporary U.S. society: the logic of self-interest and the logic of intensive mothering.

The discourse of individualism was grounded in these women's belief that it is an individual choice how to think and act, including a pregnant woman's decision about whether to drink. Because the decision is a private one, it is not anybody's else's business. This belief functions to silence communication, working against direct talk (whether interpersonal or mediated) on the subject of drinking and pregnancy. This ideology supports the general taboo reported by our sample against talking about alcohol abuse in their own families of origin and supported, as well, their general hesitancy to discuss drinking with a pregnant woman. According to the ideology of individualism, talk about drinking and pregnancy is a private matter for the woman alone to decide.

Competing with the discourse of individualism was the discourse of responsible motherhood. According to this discourse, motherhood begins with pregnancy. With motherhood comes the obligation and responsibility to place as primary the needs of the fetus. A mother who fails to do everything possible to protect her baby from risk is regarded as selfish, irresponsible, and a poor mother. According to this discourse, a mother is socially accountable for her actions. Others are given social license to hold a mother accountable for her actions, thereby granting social permission to engage in direct talk with a pregnant woman about her drinking.

The findings of the formative phase of research suggested that social-network communication on the topic of pregnancy and drinking was a complex discursive undertaking. From the logic of the discourse of individualism, it was inappropriate to develop a public health campaign that simply urged women to talk to other women about the decision to drink during pregnancy. However, the competing discourse of responsible motherhood legitimated such talk. How did our sample navigate these competing discourses? Our sample suggested that two contingencies influenced which discourse would be privileged. First, if the relationship between two women was one of family-like closeness (e.g., a mother, a close aunt, a close friend who was like a sister), then the social taboo against discussing drinking to a pregnant woman was suspended. Second, if a pregnant woman's drinking was regarded as problematic (e.g., heavy drinking as opposed to only an occasional drink), then the social taboo against talk was suspended. However, if talk was licensed, it needed to be couched in individualistic terms, underscoring the woman's choice to be a good mother.

Based on these findings from the formative phase of the project, a community-based media campaign was developed and implemented in a randomized control design (Lowe, Baxter, Hirokawa, Pearce, & Peterson, 2007). Commercial-quality materials were produced for dissemination in three channels—a broad based 30-second television commercial, a 10-minute video for localized distribution in Women, Infants, and Children (WIC) clinics, and a printed pamphlet for distribution in those clinics. To evaluate the effectiveness of the program, WIC agencies in rural Iowa were paired and randomly assigned to usual-care or intervention groups. The usual-care group was exposed only to the 30-second commercial, while the intervention group was exposed to messages in all three channels. Evaluation consisted of pre- and post-test surveys assessing two outcome variables: subject knowledge and interaction with significant people in their social milieu. Results indicated an increase in knowledge and most importantly, the multiple-channel communication increased interaction with significant others regarding the need to refrain from drinking during pregnancy.

This project illustrates how RDT can be applied during the formative phase of a planned public-health campaign to examine the meaning-making process that animates decision-making for the target population. Campaign messages were designed in order to address both of the competing discourses, in a manner consistent with how members of the target population navigated the competing discourses in their everyday lives.

Discursive Struggles in Stepfamily Communication

In a series of studies, Dawn Braithwaite and I, joined by other colleagues, have examined the competing discourses that animate communication in stepfamilies. Stepfamilies are a rapidly growing, but often problematic, family form in the U.S. (Ganong & Coleman, 2004). We have adopted a stepchild perspective in our research, to complement the adult perspective that characterizes much of the stepfamily literature.

Baxter, Braithwaite, Bryant, and Wagner (2004) conducted a qualitative interview study with young-adult stepchildren, finding that three basic discursive struggles were evident in stepparent–stepchild communication. First, stepchildren articulated an idealized discourse of closeness with the stepparent, yet at the same time they often rejected closeness with them out of a loyalty to the nonresidential parent. Second, stepchildren gave expression to a discourse of openness in their communication with the stepparent, yet at the same time they resisted such openness in favor of topic avoidance. Last, stepchildren gave expression to a discourse of legitimation of stepparent authority and discipline, yet at the same time resisted such a discourse in supporting discipline only from the residential parent or the nonresidential parent.

In the child's experience, the nonresidential parent is often positioned against the stepparent, but Braithwaite and Baxter (2006a) found that the nonresidential parent–child relationship is a discursive struggle in its own right. On the one hand, children articulated a view of the nonresidential parent as their "real" parent, yet on the other hand, they often resisted efforts by that person to enact parenting because it resulted in conflicts with the residential parent, created a sense of disloyalty to the stepparent, or simply because it disrupted daily routines in the stepfamily household. Intertwined with the first discursive struggle—a struggle surrounding the legitimation of parenting by the nonresidential parent—was the companion discursive struggle between openness and avoidance. Children embraced the ideology of openness with the nonresidential parent, yet they often avoided openness, especially on topics related to the stepparent and stepfamily life in general.

Stepchildren who live in a stepfamily household form a triadic relationship with the residential parent and the stepparent. At any given point in time as they navigate the web of discursive struggles they face, a variety of communication triads are possible (Baxter, Braithwaite, & Bryant, 2006). Stepchildren can feel like their only communicative link to the stepparent is through the residential parent (a *linked triad*); that is, the residential parent functions as a conduit, translator, or mediator between the stepparent and the stepchild. Alternatively, stepchildren can view the stepparent as a complete outsider to the residential parent–child dyad (*an outsider triad*); the stepparent is treated as an object who is present but is, for all practical purposes, communicatively ignored. Stepchildren can view themselves as the outsider against a powerful coalition between the residential parent and the stepparent in *an adult-coalition triad.* Most idealized from the stepchild perspective is *a complete triad*, in which there is open communication between all three members of the triad.

The nonresidential parent and the residential parent also face discursive struggles in stepfamilies. Schrodt, Baxter, McBride, Braithwaite, and Fine (2006) conducted a study of the meanings of the divorce decree, finding two dominant, and competing, discourses that organized everyday negotiations between coparents. RDT usefully helps us understand these systems of meaning. The discourse of the divorce decree as a legal document was characterized by a strict, legal interpretation of the divorce decree; coparents held each other to the "letter of the law" and allowed no room for variation. By contrast, the discourse of the divorce decree as guide was characterized by coparents who viewed the divorce decree as a general guide, subject to ongoing and emergent interpretation as circumstances demanded. Although some stepfamilies privileged one of these discourses over the other, the most dynamic stepfamily experience featured an ebb-and-flow pattern in which families moved in and out of these two discourses. For example, the discourse of guide was followed until one parent perceived that they were being taken advantage of, at which point a shift to the discourse of legal document gained currency. As well, the discourse of legal document proved very rigid over time, eliciting a discourse of guide with its greater capacity for adaptation to emergent family needs.

Two studies in the research program have examined the role of stepfamily ritualizing. Braithwaite, Baxter, and Harper (1998) found that successful stepfamily rituals were those that paid homage both to the "new" stepfamily as well as to the "old" family of origin. Stepfamily rituals were less meaningful if they were perceived to ignore one of these constituent family units; that is, rituals that celebrated the stepfamily but not the family of origin or rituals that celebrated the family of origin to the relative neglect of the stepfamily. Most recently, Baxter and her colleagues (Baxter et al., 2007) have examined the remarriage ceremony as a stepfamily ritual. They found that, for the most part, their young-adult stepchild informants experienced the ceremony as an empty ritual. Several reasons accounted for this, but the general overarching pattern was that the ritual failed to pay homage to the family of origin and to the newly formed stepfamily unit; instead, the ritual honored only the remarrying couple. The remarriage ceremony appears to be a missed opportunity for many stepfamilies; it holds the often unrealized potential to construct the stepfamily unit in a positive manner.

Stepchildren often feel trapped by the web of discursive struggles that animate their stepfamily experiences. Their communicative life in the stepfamily is often riddled with inconsistencies, ambivalences, mixed messages, and a general affective tone of frustration.

CONCLUSION

In this chapter, I have attempted to illustrate one approach to inter-personal/family communication that holds potential to join the interdisciplinary table with a fresh vantage point—the dialogic perspective of relational dialectics theory. The basis of that distinctiveness rests on a conceptualization of communication as an interdependence of messages, in particular a conceptualization of communication as Bakhtin's (1986, p. 93) "chain of speech communion." This theoretical perspective is social, not psychological, in that meaning-making is located in the interplay of various discourses, rather than inside the cognitive processing of individual minds. It is social, but not sociological, in that the focus is on utterances and the flux of meaning-making rather than the social structures that organize society. It is a communication perspective, one among several that have emerged over the past two decades as scholars of interpersonal/family communication have come into their own and found their unique disciplinary voice.

REFERENCES

Altman, I., & Taylor, D. (1973). *Social penetration: The development of interpersonal relationships*. New York: Holt, Rinehart, and Winston.

Bachen, C., & Illouz, E. (1996). Imagining romance: Young people's cultural models of romance and love. *Critical Studies in Mass Communication, 13*, 279–308.

Bakhtin, M. M. (1981). *The dialogic imagination: Four essays by M. M. Bakhtin* (M. Holquist, Ed.; C. Emerson, & M. Holquist, Trans.). Austin, TX: University of Texas Press.

Bakhtin, M. M. (1984). *Problems of Dostoevsky's poetics* (C. Emerson, Ed. and Trans.). Minneapolis, MN: University of Minnesota Press.

Bakhtin, M. M. (1986). *Speech genres and other late essays* (C. Emerson, & M. Holquist, Eds.; V. McGee, Trans.). Austin, TX: University of Texas Press.

Bakhtin, M. M. (1990). *Art and answerability: Early philosophical essays by M. M. Bakhtin* (M. Holquist, & V. Liapunov, Eds.; V. Liapunov & K. Brostrom, Trans.). Austin, TX: University of Texas Press.

Baxter, L. A. (1987). Symbols of relationship identity in relationship cultures. *Journal of Social and Personal Relationships, 4*, 261–280.

Baxter, L. A. (1990). Dialectical contradictions in relationship development. *Journal of Social and Personal Relationships, 7,* 69–88.

Baxter, L. A. (1992). Forms and functions of intimate play in personal relationships. *Human Communication Research, 18,* 336–363.

Baxter, L. A. (1993). "Talking things through" and "Putting it in writing": Two codes of communication in an academic institution. *Journal of Applied Communication Research, 21,* 313–326.

Baxter, L. A. (2004). Distinguished Scholar Article: Relationships as dialogues. *Personal Relationships, 11,* 1–22.

Baxter, L. A. (2006). Relational dialectics theory: Multivocal dialogues of family communication. In D. O. Braithwaite & L. A. Baxter (Eds.), *Engaging theories in family communication: Multiple perspectives* (pp. 130–145). Thousand Oaks, CA: Sage.

Baxter, L. A. (2007). Problematizing the problem in communication: A dialogic perspective. *Communication Monographs, 74,* 119–125.

Baxter, L. A., & Akkoor, C. (2006, June). *Aesthetic love and romantic love in close relationships: A case study of East Indian arranged marriages.* Paper presented to the Communication Ethics Conference, Pittsburgh, PA.

Baxter, L. A., & Babbie, E. (2004). *The basics of communication research.* Belmont, CA: Wadsworth.

Baxter, L. A., & Braithwaite, D.O. (2002). Performing marriage: The marriage renewal ritual as cultural performance. *Southern Communication Journal, 67,* 94–109.

Baxter, L. A., & Braithwaite, D. O. (2006). Family rituals. In L. H. Turner, & R. West (Eds.), *The family communication sourcebook* (pp. 259–280). Thousand Oaks, CA: Sage.

Baxter, L. A., & Braithwaite, D. O. (in press a). *Engaging theories in interpersonal communication.* Thousand Oaks, CA: Sage.

Baxter, L. A., & Braithwaite, D. O. (in press b). Relational dialectics theory: Crafting meaning from competing discourses. In L. A. Baxter, & D. O. Braithwaite (Eds.), *Engaging theories in interpersonal communication.* Thousand Oaks, CA: Sage.

Baxter, L. A., Braithwaite, D. O., & Bryant, L. E. (2006). Types of communication triads perceived by young-adult stepchildren in established stepfamilies. *Communication Studies, 57,* 381–400.

Baxter, L. A., Braithwaite, D. O., Bryant, L., & Wagner, A.(2004). Stepchildren's perceptions of the contradictions of communication with stepparents. *Journal of Social and Personal Relationships, 21,* 447–467.

Baxter, L. A., Braithwaite, D. O., Golish, T. D., & Olson, L. N. (2002). Contradictions of interaction for wives of elderly husbands with adult dementia. *Journal of Applied Communication Research, 30,* 1–26.

Baxter, L. A., Braithwaite, D. O., Koenig Kellas, J., LeClair-Underberg, C., Lamb, E., Routsong, T., & Thatcher, M. (2007). *The remarriage ritual as an empty stepfamily ritual: The perspective of young-adult stepchildren.* Paper submitted to the National Communication Association.

Baxter, L. A., & Erbert, L. (1999). Perceptions of dialectical contradictions in turning points of development in heterosexual romantic relationships. *Journal of Social and Personal Relationships, 16,* 547–569.

Baxter, L. A., Foley, M., & Thatcher, M. (2006, November). *Marginalizing difference in personal relationships: A dialogic analysis of partner talk about difference.* Paper presented at the National Communication Association Convention, San Antonio, TX.

Baxter, L. A., Hirokawa, R., Lowe, J., Pearce, L., & Nathan, P. (2004). Dialogic voices in talk about drinking and pregnancy. *Journal of Applied Communication Research, 32,* 224–248.

Baxter, L. A., Mazanec, M., Nicholson, J., Pittman, G., Smith, K., & West, L. (1997). Everyday loyalties and betrayals in personal relationships. *Journal of Social and Personal Relationships, 14,* 655–678.

Baxter, L. A., & Montgomery, B. M. (1996). *Relating: Dialogues and dialectics.* New York: The Guilford Press.

Baxter, L. A., & Pittman, G. (2001). Communicatively remembering turning points of relationship development. *Communication Reports, 14,* 1–18.

Baxter, L. A., & Simon, E. (1993). Relationship maintenance strategies and dialectical contradictions in personal relationships. *Journal of Social and Personal Relationships, 10,* 225–242.

Baxter, L. A., & West, L. (2003). Couple perceptions of their similarities and differences: A dialectical perspective. *Journal of Social and Personal Relationships, 20,* 491–514.

Baxter, L. A., & Widenmann, S. (1993). Revealing and not revealing the status of romantic relationships to social networks. *Journal of Social and Personal Relationships, 10,* 321–338.

Bellah, R. N., Madsen, R., Sullivan, W. M., Swidler, A., & Tipton, S. M. (1985). *Habits of the heart: Individualism and commitment in American life.* Berkeley, CA: University of California Press.

Braithwaite, D., & Baxter, L. A. (1995). "I do" again: The relational dialectics of renewing marriage vows. *Journal of Social and Personal Relationships, 12,* 177–198.

Braithwaite, D. O., & Baxter, L. A. (2006a). "You're my parent but you're not": Dialectical tensions in stepchildren's perceptions about communicating with the nonresidential parent. *Journal of Applied Communication Research, 34,* 30–48.

Braithwaite, D. O., & Baxter, L. A. (Eds.). (2006b). *Engaging theories in family communication: Multiple perspectives.* Thousand Oaks, CA: Sage.

Braithwaite, D. O., Baxter, L. A., & Harper, A.M. (1998). The role of rituals in the management of the dialectical tension of "old" and "new" in blended families. *Communication Studies, 48,* 101–120.

Bridge, K., & Baxter, L. A. (1992). Blended relationships: Friends as work associates. *Western Journal of Communication, 56,* 200–225.

Craig, R. T. (1999). Communication theory as a field. *Communication Theory, 9,* 119–161.

Ganong, L. H., & Coleman, M. (2004). *Stepfamily relationships: Development, dynamics, and interventions.* New York: Kluwer Academic, Plenum.

Hays, S. (1996). *The cultural contradictions of motherhood.* New Haven, CT: Yale University Press.

Lowe, J. B., Baxter, L. A., Hirokawa, R., Pearce, E., & Peterson, J. (2007). *The effects of a media campaign on knowledge and talk about alcohol use during pregnancy: A randomized trial.* Ms under review.

Moore, R. (1998). Love and limerence with Chinese characteristics: Student romance in the PRC. In V. de Munck (Ed.), *Romantic love and sexual behavior* (pp. 252–265). London: Praeger.

Myers, J., Madathil, J., & Tingle, L. (2005). Marriage satisfaction and wellness in India and the United States: A preliminary comparison of arranged marriages and marriages of choice. *Journal of Counseling and Development, 83,* 183–190.

National Institute on Alcohol Abuse and Alcoholism (2000a). *Tenth special report to the U. S. Congress on alcohol and health.* Washington, DC: NIAAA.

National Institute on Alcohol Abuse and Alcoholism (2000b). Fetal alcohol exposure and the brain. *Alcohol Alert, 50,* 1–4.

Penman, R. (2000). *Reconstructing communicating: Looking to a future.* Mahwah, NJ: Erlbaum.

Sahlstein, E., & Baxter, L. A. (2001). Improvising commitment in close relationships: A relational dialectics perspective. In J. H. Harvey, & A. E. Wenzel (Eds.), *Close romantic relationships: Maintenance and enhancement* (pp. 115–132). Mahwah, NJ: Erlbaum.

Schrodt, P., Baxter, L. A., McBride, M. C., Braithwaite, D. O., & Fine, M. A. (2006). The divorce decree, communication, and the structuration of coparenting relationships. *Journal of Social and Personal Relationships, 25,* 741–759.

Todorov, T. (1984). *Mikhail Bakhtin: The dialogical principle* (W. Godzich, Trans.). Minneapolis, MN: University of Minnesota Press.

SUGGESTED READINGS

Philosophical Assumptions, Secondary Sources

Baxter, L. A. (2007). Mikhail Bakhtin: The philosophy of dialogism. In P. Arneson (Ed.), *Perspectives on philosophy of communication* (pp. 247–268). West Lafayette, IN: Purdue University Press.

Holquist, M. (2002). *Dialogism* (2nd ed.). New York: Routledge.

Philosophical Assumptions, Primary Sources

Bakhtin, M. M. (1981). *The dialogic imagination: Four essays by M. M. Bakhtin* (M. Holquist, Ed.; C. Emerson, & M. Holquist, Trans.). Austin, TX: University of Texas Press.

Bakhtin, M. M. (1986). *Speech genres and other late essays* (C. Emerson & M. Holquist, Eds.; V. McGee, Trans.). Austin, TX: University of Texas Press.

Theory

Baxter, L. A. (2004). Distinguished Scholar Article: Relationships as dialogues. *Personal Relationships, 11*, 1–22.

Baxter, L. A., & Braithwaite, D. O. (in press). Relational dialectics theory: Crafting meaning from competing discourses. In L. A. Baxter, & D. O. Braithwaite (Eds.), *Engaging theories in interpersonal communication.* Thousand Oaks, CA: Sage.

Baxter, L. A., & Montgomery, B. M. (1996). *Relating: Dialogues and dialectics.* New York: The Guilford Press.

Methodology

Bakhtin, M. M. (1984). *Problems of Dostoevsky's poetics* (C. Emerson, Ed. and Trans.). Minneapolis, MN: University of Minnesota Press.

White, P. R. R. (2003). Beyond modality and hedging: A dialogic view of the language of intersubjective stance. *Text, 23*, 259–284.

Applications

Baxter, L. A., Braithwaite, D. O., Bryant, L., & Wagner, A. (2004). Stepchildren's perceptions of the contradictions of communication with stepparents. *Journal of Social and Personal Relationships, 21*, 447–467.

Baxter, L. A., Hirokawa, R., Lowe, J., Pearce, L., & Nathan, P. (2004). Dialogic voices in talk about drinking and pregnancy. *Journal of Applied Communication Research, 32*, 224–248.

Braithwaite, D.O., Baxter, L.A., & Harper, A.M. (1998). The role of rituals in the management of the dialectical tension of "old" and "new" in blended families. *Communication Studies, 48*, 101–120.

3

POLITICALLY ATTENTIVE RELATIONAL CONSTRUCTIONISM (PARC)
Making a Difference in a Pluralistic, Interdependent World

Stanley Deetz

This is my fifth time to explicitly reflect on and write my sense of the potential distinctive contribution of communication studies (Deetz, 1994, 1997a, 1997b; Deetz & Putnam 2001). I will draw some but sparingly on these earlier attempts. The 15 years provided time to think about my earlier thoughts and look at what has changed in the field.

Disappointments stand out. The "successful" textbooks as they enter into their 6th to nth editions still present communication studies as largely derivative on the theories of others, topically focused, fragmented, and reviewish. Few challenge dominant conceptions in our society and few engage real social problems. We touch the lives of hundreds of thousands of students each year with materials that are intellectually and conceptually dated and that usually only marginally or topically address issues of pluralism, globalization, mediation, corporativism, culture production, community development, and public decision-making—all issues that make communication central to human concerns and choices that are core to the very life of contemporary democratic society. What are the systems of choice, preparation, and economics that keep producing these outcomes?

Excitement is also present. Many of the best scholars of the field are addressing social issues and problems rather than simply contributing to the topic-centered literatures of our field. And, with that, funding and recognition are greatly increasing. The contributions to health communication and health campaigns have put communication scholars in important policy decision contexts. The study of discourse in a variety of contexts has been greatly impacted by communication scholars. Communication scholars are contributing greatly to understanding media and popular culture and are deeply involved in communication policy discussions. With these contributions have come leadership roles and citations of our works, and improvements in intellectual discussions and society more widely.

And frustrations. Other disciplines are being greatly impacted by communication theories, though many of these are not developed by individuals who are seen as in communication studies. One can easily be dismayed with how slow our field has been to take seriously the linguistic turn in philosophy where human interaction replaced human consciousness as the central issue spawning new conceptions and theories across the social sciences and humanities. The vast majority of our field sat back while English departments in virtually every type of institution took seriously the implication of text theory and postmodernist philosophy. They became "communication" theorists before most in our field. Psychologists, sociologists, and family therapists built largely social constructionism, while most in communication department sat back reproducing older psychological reductionisms. Clearly exceptions and important formative contributions exist (see Jackson, Poole & Kuhn, 2002; Leeds-Hurwitz, 1995; McNamee & Gergen, 1999; Pearce, 1989, 2008; Pearce & Cronen, 1980; Shotter, 1993; Shotter & Gergen, 1994) but they were often marginalized.

I'm not saying that we should have uncritically accepted these new ways of thinking about (or better through) communication, maybe not even that we should have/could have developed them. The biggest problem was that many of the rank and file of our field sat on the sidelines unable/unwilling to enter the debates. Our courses remained devoid of the most original and conceptually challenging communication theories. Communication textbooks and courses appear to do a lot of reviews of literatures and definitions of terms, but rarely work from an integrated theory, or have worked little with interaction process explanations and the constitutive processes of communication. And even a quick survey of our textbooks shows the most popular to be totally out of touch with the larger debates around "our" perspective. As a field we have embraced many disciplines' *theories of communication* but not attended much to *communication theories* (see Deetz, 1994; Deetz & Radford, in press). The issue here is not that we often think of ourselves as second rate and by extension treat our own best minds as derivative; or that we cite work from other disciplines more often then they cite us or we ourselves. The issue for me is that we are not active, and don't ask our students to be active, in engaging in the invention of conceptions and practices necessary for the problems and hopes of our time.

In this chapter I wish to show that the world community is experiencing a set of new situations and problems for which particular communication theories provide useful conceptions and responses. Members of the field of communication have developed fairly sophisticated communication theories that can be very valuable in addressing them. I will describe these generally as based on a kind of politically attentive relational constructionism (PARC). But we have to move these theories in from the margins if we are to provide our critical social contribution.

In many ways this chapter works at a more fundamental, radical level than others in this volume. It aims at reframing our enterprise rather than developing a part of it. This is not to argue against other valuable work other members of the field do, or that done in other fields, but to say that communication scholars and teachers have an important distinctive contribution to make that is different from this. And the impact of even current work would be greater if it were articulated in relation to these newer theories. Unfortunately we have been slow in doing this. Our new social context is one of those historical moments that requires a new professional and everyday vocabulary for attending to and talking about social and material world (see White, 1983). The chapter will focus on the social science parts of the field, though I have, in a distant past, tried to apply similar ideas to rhetoric and the oral interpretation of literature (Deetz, 1984, 1983; and see authors like Deluca, 1999).

THE SOCIAL CONTEXT FOR OUR CONTRIBUTION

Most today accept some version of Thomas Kuhn's insight that new paradigms arise around a significant anomalous finding that dominant paradigms treat in some fashion but nonetheless remains as a kind of glitch for prevailing theories. A new paradigm arrives on the scene that is able to solve or reconfigure the anomaly. The new paradigm, in providing a way of handling this anomaly, in turn offers interesting and productive ways to handle other things that were thought solved by dominant perspectives. In the social sciences we have tended to work somewhat differently from this. Our dominant paradigms more often change around new/emerging social conditions and social needs, and the development of interesting and compelling new ways to think and talk about these.

Core disciplines in the social sciences came into being addressing an emergent central issue in society. In doing so they were based not so much on a body of findings initially but provide a compelling way to talk about, think about, and address the new issue. As such, they provided everyday people new ways to think and talk about critical concerns. They shifted native, everyday, theories, and they work generatively in Gergen's (1978; see Deetz, 2008) sense.

For example, psychology both drew attention to and grew out of concern with the hidden forces of individual behavior and benefited from a society looking to better predict and control people (Rose, 1990). And sociology both drew attention to and grew out of concern with hidden forces of societal forms, and benefited from fear of disorder as people moved from communities to societies. Both have become part of the wider social discourse leading to, at one time, new ways of thinking about social and personal life. Unfortunately, their metaphors have been reified into properties of people and society and this has led to predictable social misrecognitions and responses. In many respects these two disciplines helped make (or satisfied a social desire for) the development of new forms of social control, integration, cultural management, and normalization—all hallmarks of the 20th century. But the current need for simultaneous economic, social, and ecological sustainability requires invention and creativity based on difference rather than order and control. This is a need that the dominant orientations did not provide for. The Latin root of communication "to make common" draws our attention away from our need for difference and to invent together. The Roman worldview based on systems of centrality, superiority, and control may lead us away from the more cosmopolitan view of the Greeks.

The 21st-century challenges to the 20th-century orientations are everywhere. Globalization, pluralism, ecological crises, respect for difference, awareness that we all live downstream, the loss of certainties, the consequences of a neoliberal world order, and so on and so forth foster an atmosphere demanding greater abilities to make collaborative decisions across personal/social/cultural difference. We are at a kind of crossroads where we can choose to develop larger and more powerful systems of integration and control or foster a more robust form of democracy where we more productively gain from our differences. Communication theories can contribute to either but for reasons sketched below, though beyond the scope of this chapter, I believe that contribution to the latter is more important and distinct in contribution. We are asked to make a communication response to the useful descriptions in Ben Barber's *Jihad Versus McWorld* (1995) or Al Gore's *Assault on Reason* (2007).

In many respects, contemporary society has gotten caught in dualities and oscillations—objectivism/subjectivism, secular humanism integrated by market economy/religious traditionalism integrated by core values—without understanding that communication potentially provides a "third way" of productively making decisions together with our differences. Political discussion and joint decision-making have been devalued partly because we do them so badly, and we do them badly lacking the communication concepts and practices to do them well in our contemporary context (Deetz & Irvin, 2008; Varey, 2002).

This is a significant time for communication scholars. People throughout the world have to respond to fundamentally new social, economic, and political issues. Not surprisingly, the public decisions that influence everyday lives appear increasingly beyond everyday people's reach, outside the realm of democratic processes, beyond even lingering hopes for control, or reached in dysfunctional political institutions. The resultant political apathy, cynicism, bullhorn expressionism, and self-centered opportunism serve as understandable if dangerous dominant attitudes of our times. If we are to rekindle a faith in our capacity to work together to produce the future we want, we must ask fundamental questions about where significant decisions are made and how the processes of making these decisions can be made more effective and democratic. These are at root communication questions, but I do not think we, nor the general public, have thought them through terribly well, especially as communication questions, for a number of reasons.

For example, we have tended to join with the various commercial sponsors to focus on the more superficial phenomenon, the rapid technological advances in information and mediated communication. Certainly the changes here are significant and we should engage them directly. They should not be left to vendors, engineers, and cognitive psychologists. But, despite all the hype about the information revolution, cyberspace, and teleconnectedness, the challenges we face today are much more fundamental and difficult. The loss of stable communities, shared values, and spaces for public proactive creative decision-making is often the hidden side of the rapid advances in transportation, computer and data transmission capacities, the globalization of business, and the mass-mediated world. Unfortunately, especially in the case of developments in information technologies, more attention has been given to electronic connectedness, information diffusion and data-sharing potentials without attending to the need for new developments in social relations and communities and higher-order forms of social knowledge.

Even worse, those valorizing the "information" society are often participants in a veiled attack on the public sphere and the capacity for public discussion and collective decision-making. Marketplace decisions made by individuals in private spaces represent very different interests than their political voice in public decision processes. Public discussion is often replaced by rapidly reproduced opinions and information stripped of human situations, emotions, processes, and awareness of economic sponsorship. Thoughts and knowledge that in democracies arise out of conflicting experiences, interpretations, and alternative choice possibilities are often replaced by commercially produced and massively reproduced knowledge artifacts.

In the proclamation of the information age, information has been treated as a neutral commodity and communication reduced to acts of transmission. The important processes of mediation are treated as neutral and transparent. The human problems communication scholars must address today are not answered by more information but by providing people with the places and the means for productively resolving conflicts and making choices together. Al Gore may be right that information technologies offer possibilities but only if they are understood in larger communication and community terms.

What is radical about our new social context from a communication standpoint is not the rapid expansion of global public information but the breakdown of the walls of homogeneous communities and the various types of consensus on which their decisions and talk were based. The presence of unexpected and often undesired diversity creates a problem for the traditional world, but also tremendous opportunity (see Deetz & Radford, in press). In a diverse social context, the traditional cultural assumptions are seen as only one type of social arrangement—an arrangement and set of assumptions that can be maintained through control or can be open to negotiation. Communication practices designed to speak from our consensus, from an identity, about knowledge are not necessarily useful when we have to talk to create and work out these things in the contemporary world.

Today our most basic social question is: Given that we live together in an increasingly interdependent world where most of the things we once took for granted are now open to constant renegotiations, negotiations that require human interactions but are often contrived in unproductive ways, how are we to make satisfying and just decisions together? Communication studies could provide a productive way of addressing this question. Unfortunately our conceptions of quality communication, like the native theories of larger publics, are linked to more basic 18th-century conceptions of personal experience and individual psychology loosely held together with the acceptance of liberal democracy ideals of free speech and the marketplace of ideas—a particular kind of democracy, as Barber suggests, that was designed more to keep us safely apart than productively together (see Barber, 1984).

Such ideals were supported by particular conceptions of meaning, people, language, and social relations that are no longer tenable and that often lead us astray in attempts to make better joint decisions. Many have taken seriously the need to get people together in the room, but most have not attended well to what we do once we are there. A fundamentally 18th-century theory of communication is not likely to provide for the needs of a 21st-century society and the collaborative processes necessary to live productively together. The domination by psychological ways of thinking and individualism can severely limit our ability to do better.

Most of the Western conceptions of communication and governance that were contained in the U.S. Declaration of Independence—concepts of expression, natural rights of individuals, freedoms from—were fine for independent shop owners and farmers with an open horizon of space and natural resources. But the same ideas can lead to bad decisional processes in a pluralistic, interdependent world. We await a suitable Declaration of Interdependence—with concepts of collaboration, community rights, and freedoms in-order-to—articulated within 21st- rather than 18th-century conceptions of the person, communication and governance. This is required, I believe, if we are to create businesses, communities, and a world that is economically, ecologically, and socially sustainable. Jefferson would have written things differently with a factory hog farm up the road and with contemporary understandings of the communication process.

Characterizing our time as an age of negotiation and collaboration and developing constructionist conceptions heightens our understanding of the social problems and opportunities we face today. Communication scholars can continue to reproduce 18th-century conceptions and "band aid" the problems or lead in the development of fundamentally new conceptions of meaning, people, language, and social relations. Life circumstances have given us problems that our native and professional concepts of communication and democracy were not designed to address.

Our situation is not unique in the social sciences, as Nadeau recently stated regarding economics:

> The origins of neoclassical economics in mid-19th century physics were forgotten. Subsequent generations of mainstream economists accepted the claim that this theory is scientific . . . If the environmental crises did not exist, the fact that neoclassical economic theory provides a coherent basis for managing economic activities in market systems could be viewed as sufficient justification for its widespread applications. But because the crises do exist, this theory can no longer be regarded as useful even in pragmatic and utilitarian terms . . . Because neoclassical economic theory does not even acknowledge the cost of environmental problems and the limits to economic growth, it constitutes one of the greatest barriers to combating climate change and other threats to the planet. (2008, 42)

POLITICALLY ATTENTIVE RELATIONAL CONSTRUCTIONISM (PARC)

Fortunately, since the 1960s a radical new set of communication concepts has been developed that, if continued in development and partly redirected, offers great promise to reinvigorate democracy, and to make understanding communication processes core to everyone's understanding of social life. Growing out of the "linguistic turn" in philosophy in the 1930s and aided by social ferment and the public's vague understanding of the politics of the personal in the 1960s, the emerging social constructionist, critical, and poststructuralist concepts placed communication processes as constitutive of the personal and the social. In communication studies, some of this has gradually been pulled together in various places and institutionalized in the social constructionism division of the national association (Leeds-Hurwitz, 1995). But the importance is greater than just another interest area.

This is a radical, "big" idea—a new general paradigm—requiring sophisticated conceptions of communication and providing a fundamental challenge to commonsense thinking. I consider this to be as big as the social conditions and resultant new conceptions of persons and social relations that congealed as liberal democracy in the 18th century. In this, I believe, rests the possibility of a distinct and crucial contribution of communication education and scholarship.

Cultural studies in mass communication, critical studies in organizational communication and feminist theory generally have made some of these theories mainstay in their areas, but these have at times remained esoteric and have often done more to criticize existing social formations and decision processes than to invent new ones. But in these hope and conceptual power exist.

Collectively I have characterized these diverse works as a *politically attentive relational constructionism* (PARC). I use relational rather than social constructionism to avoid connection to a commonly mis-understood position and to draw attention to more fundamental relational processes of the person-in-the-world-with-others-moving-toward-a-future/past. Studying the hyphens and hyphenated is central. Experience, meaning, the very objects of our world arise out of rela-tions and lose sense outside them (Deetz 2000; Gergen, 1994). And these relational formations are deeply political.

I believe that PARC theories do not provide simply more perspec-tives for the field, they provide a way to rethink people, interaction, and social life in a distinctly communicative way. As part of a paradigmatic shift they offer new possibilities in rethinking everything from public relations and campaigns to families and intimate relationships. Some of these areas have been developed more than others. And the number of developing communication theories within this larger paradigm is fairly large.

All of these various works begin with a basic relational construction-ism. Basic principles are widely shared among theorists from many camps though theorists differ in their relative emphasis on the pheno-menological, social, material, and political. Shared conceptions include: perception and experience arise in the specific ways that they do based on a relational encounter with the world, others, social forms, and our own interiors. Perception originates from a standpoint or subject pos-ition; standpoints and subject positions are social and systemic rather than personal, psychological, or subjective (see Deetz, 1992; Weedon, 1997). Thus, the social and historical precedes the personal. Studying the communication processes that produce the person in particular ways enables understandings and insights that studying communication as personal expressions of a psychological being does not. Knowledge, facts, and social order are outcomes of communicative processes rather than existing independently to be represented. As such things become institutionalized, they are experienced as presocial realities and the processes of production, and their politics, are overlooked or hidden. Psychological, sociological, and even mental "states" are often more usefully seen as products of communication processes rather than as causes of them. Language is not a device for representation but an essential part of the production of the "objects" to be represented.

Since power is ever present and relational construction is a historical process, politics is everywhere and intrinsic to our experiences, identities, knowledge, information, values, institutions, and so forth. A central issue for study is how to make these constitutive political processes visible and more democratic. And with this arises a concern with the relational nature of being and "otherness." The recovery of conflict and otherness—the difference, outside, and not yet determined—rather than understanding the self, reflection, and empathy become the central driving forces of productive interaction and decision-making (for example, see Ashcraft & Mumby, 2004; Deetz, 1990; Pinchevski, 2005).

PARC thus goes beyond casual versions of constructionism. Most scholars, including those in communication studies, accept some version of constructionism. But acceptance and practice are not always the same. Many, if not most, appear to work analogous to a person who believes that the earth is round but operates day-to-day as if it were flat. Perhaps flat earth assumptions are routinely okay since assuming curvature often only makes most calculations more difficult without much utility. But at critical times and places remembering that it is round and being able to work with curvature matters a lot. Following the analogy, our contemporary social context makes PARC matter a lot. Flat earth-like assumptions of communication in a homogeneous society had utility even as they covered up much but contemporary heterogeneous societies require much more. Which version of constructionism—whether developed from hermeneutics, critical theory, poststructuralism, feminism, articulation theory, or Wittengenstein—matters less than the serious acceptance of some version.

Many of the so-called communication theories in the field are actually mid to lower level accounts of particular interaction phenomena explained by forces that are considered before or beneath communication. These "theories" often rest on a set of implicit or implied, but weakly explicated, more general common-sense theories of the person and human experience. Most often these implicit general theories are based on an everyday version of psychological reductionism and connected to a humanist agenda and liberal democracy. Since such a view is widely shared, it often remains invisible and undiscussed. Such a view is part of "our" common sense and shared with our students and outside constituent groups but has costs to them and us.

PARC is not just another perspective or midrange theory within this tradition but challenges this undiscussed consensus. For this reason, developing PARC studies often require engaging larger theoretical issues and the development of a number of new concepts, conceptions often not already present in our language, simply to discover what the studies do. This challenges our teaching and our students but makes communication studies more than commonsense, and in ways that are critical to living together in the contemporary world.

AN EXAMPLE OF A UNIQUE CONTRIBUTION

Communication scholars need to enrich the concepts and practices of communication to aid society. Those working from PARC are making many novel contributions. Here I will show implications from a communication-enriched critical theory, though similar contributions could come from other PARC perspectives. I will highlight the themes my work picks up. But many other parallel lines of work are present highlighting other issues. My concern is not so much which line of work is followed as that we take seriously a new way to think about our field and its unique possibilities.

Jürgen Habermas (1984, 1987) is to be credited with developing one of the most complete communication theories of the 20th century. His attempts to revitalize the public sphere and ground ethics and morally-guided human development in open communicative processes rather than external substantive foundations are well known in the field. His carefully developed and detailed distinction between "strategic communication" and "communication in the pursuit of mutual understanding" was a theoretically grounded understanding of what was mostly a superficial fight between those in the field who saw all communication as an attempt at influence and those promoting dialogue. But the relationships to Habermas's work should not be seen as a one-way street. Much of the consequence of his communication theory is yet to be worked out and many of the limits of Habermas's approach arise from him as a philosopher not knowing enough about interaction systems to carry it through to our contemporary needs. To the extent that we share his democratic impulse over extending strategic control, he has provided a helpful beginning.

Strategic Communication and Systematically Distorted Communication

First, Habermas's conception of various forms of strategy in communication and especially his conception of the double blind strategic nature of systematically distorted communication provides a basis for careful exploration of various interaction system pathologies and how individuals unwittingly consent to them (see Ganesh, Zoller, & Cheney, 2005; Jian, 2007; Thackaberry, 2004, for example). We might expect, at some point, that the field will pay much attention to the structural and systemic bases of discursive closure and systematically distorted communication as we have in the past to persuasion, influence, and logical fallacies. The nonintentional and nonpsychological descriptions provide the bases for a communication explanation of numerous individual and social difficulties.

Going beyond Habermas, from a number of different perspectives and expressed in different ways, communication scholars are making contributions to studies of more subtle forms of strategic communication. Cultural studies' focus on the production of wants and consumption culture through mass media has been very important work. Much of the work on the production of personal identities provides new insights into the social and contrived nature of any particular personage (Holmer-Nadesan, 1997).

Rethinking Free Speech and General Symmetry Conditions

Second, Habermas's conception of the general symmetry conditions of open communication provides a basis for developing a productive democracy's need for all relevant positions to be heard, rather than the individual bases for free expression. Such a conception makes "megaphone size"—the access and ability to "broadcast" messages—rather than simply free speech a relevant consideration for open communication at all levels, whether it be political processes, work team meetings, or relational development. Despite the everyday focus on having a "say," freedom of speech as a social principle for democracy is a necessary, but certainly not sufficient, condition. If the interior is formed in conditions of asymmetry, the ability to freely express provides little. In relational constructionism, democracy exists or does not in the systems of construction rather than expression, and "voice" relates to open processes of meaning construction rather than free expression of formed meanings. But it remains to communication scholars to detail how requisite diversity and process rules recover democracy's potential for mutual productive decisions from the limits of argumentation, deliberation, representation and everyone having a say (see Deetz & Irvin, 2008; Varey, 2002).

Further, Habermas develops a foundation for looking at the specific conditions where strategic communication is redeemable. Clearly morally suspect strategic communication often occurs in contemporary society and communication professionals have been active is enabling particular groups' advantage through it. Still, communication scholars can add much to detail the situations where strategic communication leads to distortions and, in contrast, where it can open the possibility of a more open and productive discourse.

Free and Open Development Through Contestation

And, third, Habermas provided an analytic account of arenas of human difference and spaces of contestation as well as a beginning description of how domination and closure of contestation occur. All communication makes claims about our inner world, the external world, and social relations as well as other things. These he described as claims of *truthfulness* (sincerity), *truth*, and *propriety*. Our field has done much looking at the influence of these claims. What Habermas does is lead us to look beyond the effect of claims to the different forms of social/relational grounding.

Contestation and Truthfulness   "Truthfulness"—the relation of a claim to our insides—for example, can be problematic for Habermas not because we are psychologically misguided or "truthiness" prevails but because our interiors—thoughts and emotions—are active relational products, products often produced in conditions of asymmetry. The question for a communication scholar is not whether we can figure out what we really feel and clearly express it, but whether we can reclaim indeterminacy and create open creative reformation. These both require greater encounter with variety and difference. "Difference" or "distantiation," rather than the humanistic processes of reflection and self-understanding, are essential to open self-/other-formation. This requires a sophisticated understanding of the politics of experience and language that runs counter to self-evidentness and sense of owned personal experience as well as the psychological accounts of deception and self-deception. An understanding of the communication processes makes a distinct contribution to this set of complex issues. This contribution is critical to understanding the forces of cultural management and to productively encounter social difference.

Contestation and Truth   The concern with the expression and adjudication of different knowledge claims—the relation of claim to the external world—gets a new and more powerful meaning for communication scholars in this new formulation. We as a society are often caught between trying to reach certainty and treating everything as an opinion. Even our professional work often retains this duality. Relational constructionism generally and standpoint theory specifically have opened a large space between those two. The new challenge is to open the knowledge construction processes to contestation, not to get it right but to complicate knowledge. Doing so begins to reclaim knowledge from the popular focus on information—information stripped from the nature of its production. The politics of knowledge and information can be reclaimed as a legitimate value discussion rather than left as being right or everyone's opinion counts equally (Deetz, 2000). Such potential is essential for a global community having to make complicated, interdependent, social, and environmental choices.

Contestation and Social Relations   While Habermas was more concerned with claims and general issues of social order and rules, for communication scholars, the politics of identity has become a central way that contestation over social relations is occurring. This is comprehensible if we understand identity in relational terms—for me to be an "x" requires that you will be a "y." Rights and obligations are entailed with the very subject position(s) one takes on (or takes on us) in an interaction system. We know that many armed conflicts around the world are based on identity issues and for this reason are often, unlike resource conflicts, considered intractable. Much of this results from treating the outcomes of relational construction as fixed, with talk originating from them, rather than entering into the discussion at the level of construction. Pearce and Littlejohn (1999) are among the few to describe the nature and consequences of the manner of communication and the construction process. Again the space for a communication contribution as an investigation of how we come to think and talk about ourselves in particular ways would enable a more productive engagement of these situations (see Pearce, 2007). The issues of gender politics are of course obviously of consequence here too. Communication scholars have already started making important contributions here (see Ashcraft & Mumby, 2004, for example).

Moving Beyond Habermas with Communication Theory

Anyone familiar with Habermas already knows that I have given his work a distinctive communication framing here that takes this work well outside his philosophical project. Along these lines we can continue to build a general communication theory that would help us address the contemporary social context and its difficulties.

Many agree that Habermas's approach is weakened based on his emphasis on consensus—"reaching common understanding"—through appeals in discourse and contestation to prior, more basic, consensus (e.g., Benhabib, 1992; Young, 1996). With this, his conceptual use of argument theory rather than interactional process theories is understandable but limiting.

In this sense his work pushes toward deliberative processes, where we reason to conclusions, or dialogue, where we try to understand each other. Our need today is not so much for common understanding as for commitment to a joint course of action that enables us to productively live in the world together. Because of the reflective turn he takes, Habermas is limited in consideration of the possibility of creative production in interaction. "Getting to yes," for example, uses conflict to produce rather than overcome conflict by that held in common (Fisher & Ury, 1981). This productivity was something already shown in Heidegger through Gadamer as implicit in the linguistic turn because of a strong conception of the "other." Habermas under-appreciates conflict and the possibilities of human creativity because he does not see contestation and deconstruction—the recovery of the indeterminant from its various determination—as aiding invention. This is exactly what a stronger communication theory enables. But of course Habermas is not alone, the same difficulty cripples the liberal democratic political processes in our new context of pluralism and interdependence.

MAKING THE CONTRIBUTION REAL

Unlike mid-range theories that tend to stay at a middle level regarding a rather narrow domain, PARC tends to work back and forth between general theories of society and concrete situated human practices (e.g., Broadfoot, 2008; Dempsey, 2007). We are gradually developing the conceptions and practices of dialogue and collaborative talk that, when connected with a more powerfully analytic conceptual frame like that of Habermas, are used to enrich the democratic processes at a variety of levels (Deetz & Irvin, 2008). Significant impactful work is being done in communities (Forester, 1999; Pearce & Pearce, 2001). Communication may better be about transformation through invention than as empathy and dialogue; the better image is a triangle led by the relation to the outside than interaction between people.

Such understandings can easily be extended to engage in much larger projects of environmentally sensitive development and nation-building. Other countries are taking stakeholder relationship and collaborative decision-making much more seriously than we currently are (see Cruz, Pedrozo, Bacima, & Queiroz, 2007; Roper, Zorn, & Weaver, 2004). They are rethinking communication and various democratic institutions and their implied communications models. Much potential is seen in public/private collaborations, though studies have found these often hampered by an ethos of "everyone having a say" and more generally of liberal democratic native theories of communication (Heath, 2005; MacDonald, 2004). Much of the work on organizations and stakeholder-based decision-making is turning to new communication theories but is still often hampered by not taking communication seriously enough (Deetz, 2007). Cultural studies scholars have done much to detail the processes of cultural reproduction and domination and are beginning to develop communication system interventions that lead to the more open formation of meaning.

CONCLUSION

Communication studies show more distinctive qualities and make a greater contribution when scholars write less to each other about communication topics and join in more with others to solve human problems. In the two largest projects with which I am currently affiliated—one based on a US$5 million gift (now expanded to US$20 million) to transform science education in North America and the other a five-year NSF project to advance the careers of women in the sciences—I was asked to join for my expertise in organizational change and development, but the contribution I have made links more to the issues above. Knowledge and identity politics matter a lot in these projects; communication theory provides the best opportunity to understand and engage these politics. The native theories of psychology and democracy often get in the way of understanding the complex dynamics occurring. People support getting stakeholders to the table but are not very good at understanding the processes that occur once they are there. And, all too often as good thoughtful members of our time, they describe the problems in people and personality terms, thus overlooking the complex interactional dynamics that have people and personality as one of their outcomes. We have a distinctive contribution to make here.

But the most basic contribution does not come in the specific things we do but in the way we help society to think communicationally. I can imagine a time when everyday people can think interaction patterns and systematically distorted communication as easily as they currently think about personality and social class. Where difference will be seen as an opportunity to overcome unwitting consent to large systems of cultural management and invention rather than a problem to be managed or tolerated. I can even imagine a rekindled faith in democracy and political processes. But all these depend on communication scholars and teachers doing their distinctive work.

REFERENCES

Ashcraft, K. L., & Mumby, D. K. (2004). *Reworking gender: A feminist communicology of organization.* Thousand Oaks, CA: Sage.

Barber, B. (1984). *Strong democracy*. Berkeley, CA: University of California Press.

Barber, B. (1995). *Jihad Versus McWorld*. New York: Times Books.

Benhabib, S. (1992). *Situating the self: Gender, community, and postmodernism in contemporary ethics*. New York: Routledge.

Broadfoot, K. (2008). *Living with genetics: Recombining self and health in modern medicine*. Cresskill, NJ: Hampton Press.

Cruz, L., Pedrozo, E., Bacima, R., & Queiroz, B. (2007). Company and society: The "Caras do Brasil" (Faces of Brazil) program as leverage for sustainable development. *Management Decision, 45/8*, 1297–1319.

Deetz, S. (1983). Review essay: Negation and the political function of rhetoric. *Quarterly Journal of Speech, 69*, 434–441.

Deetz, S. (1984). The politics of the oral interpretation of literature. *Literature in Performance, 4*, 60–64.

Deetz, S. (1990). Reclaiming the subject matter as a guide to mutual understanding: Effectiveness and ethics in interpersonal interaction. *Communication Quarterly, 38*, 226–243.

Deetz, S. (1992). *Democracy in an age of corporate colonization: Developments in communication and the politics of everyday life*. Albany, NY: State University of New York Press.

Deetz, S. (1994). The future of the discipline: The challenges, the research, and the social contribution. In S. Deetz (Ed.). *Communication yearbook 17* (pp. 565–600). Thousand Oaks, CA: Sage.

Deetz, S. (1997a). Communication in an age of negotiation: International Communication Association presidential address. *Journal of Communication, 47*, 118–135.

Deetz, S. (1997b). The contribution of communication studies to the emerging age of negotiation. *Florida Communication Journal, 25*, 11–23.

Deetz, S. (2000). Putting the community into organizational science: Exploring the construction of knowledge claims. *Organization Science, 11*, 732–738.

Deetz, S. (2007). Corporate governance, communication and CRS. In S. May, G. Cheney, & J. Roper (Eds.), *The debate over corporate social responsibility* (pp. 267–278). Oxford: Oxford University Press.

Deetz, S. (2008). Engagement as co-generative theorizing. *Journal of Applied Communication Research, 36*, 288–296.

Deetz, S., & Irvin, L. (2008). Governance, stakeholder involvement and new communication models. In S. Odugbemi, & T. Jacobson (Eds.) *Governance reform under real world conditions: Citizens, stakeholders, and voice* (pp. 163–180). Washington, DC: The World Bank.

Deetz, S., & Putnam, L. (2001). Thinking about the future of communication studies. In W. Gudykunst (Ed.), *Communication yearbook 24* (pp. 2–15). Thousand Oaks, CA: Sage.

Deetz, S., & Radford, G. (in press). *Communication theory at the crossroads: Theorizing for globalization, pluralism and collaboration*. Oxford: Blackwell Publications.

Deluca, K. (1999). Articulation theory: A discursive grounding for rhetorical practice. *Philosophy and Rhetoric, 32,* 334–347.

Dempsey, S. (2007) Negotiating accountability within international contexts: The role of bounded voice. *Communication Monographs, 74,* 311–332.

Fisher, R., & Ury, W. (1981). *Getting to yes.* New York: Penguin Books.

Forester, J. (1999). *The deliberative practitioner: Encouraging participatory planning processes.* Cambridge, MA: MIT Press.

Ganesh, S., Zoller, H. M., & Cheney, G. (2005). Transforming resistance, broadening our boundaries: Critical organizational communication meets globalization from below. *Communication Monographs, 72,* 169–191.

Gergen, K. J. (1978). Toward generative theory. *Journal of Personality and Social Psychology, 31,* 1344–1360.

Gergen, K. J. (1994). *Realities and relationships.* Cambridge, MA: Harvard University Press.

Gore, A. (2007). *The assault on reason.* New York: Penguin Books.

Habermas, J. (1984). *The theory of communicative action:* Vol. 1 *Reason and the rationalization of society* (Trans. T. McCarthy). Boston: Beacon Press.

Habermas, J. (1987). *The theory of communicative action:* Vol. 2 *Lifeworld and system* (Trans. T. McCarthy). Boston: Beacon Press.

Heath, R. (2005). *Interorganizational collaboration: Implications for democracy in community models of communication and problem solving.* Unpublished doctoral dissertation, University of Colorado, Boulder, Co.

Holmer-Nadesan, M. (1997). Constructing paper dolls: The discourse of personality testing in organizational practice. *Communication Theory, 7,* 189–218.

Jackson, M. H., Poole, M. S., & Kuhn, T. (2002). The social construction of technology in studies of the workplace. In L. Lievrouw, & S. Livingstone (Eds.), *Handbook of new media: Social shaping and consequences of ICTs* (pp. 236–253). London: Sage.

Jian, G. (2007). "Omega is a four-letter word": Toward a tension-centered model of resistance to information and communication technologies. *Communication Monographs, 74,* 517–540.

Leeds-Hurwitz, W. (Ed.) (1995). *Social approaches to communication.* New York: Guilford Press.

MacDonald, J. (2004). *Public involvement in dispersing public funds: Values, native communication theories and collaboration.* Unpublished doctoral dissertation, University of Colorado, Boulder, Co.

McNamee, S., & Gergen, K. J. (Eds.). (1999). *Relational responsibility: Resources for sustainable dialogue.* Thousands Oaks, CA: Sage.

Nadeau, R. (2008). The economist has no clothes. *Scientific American,* April, p. 42.

Pearce, W. B. (1989). *Communication and the human condition.* Carbondale, IL: Southern Illinois University Press.

Pearce, W. B. (2007). *Making social worlds.* Oxford: Blackwell.

Pearce, W. B., & Cronen, V. E. (1980). *Communication, action and meaning: The creation of social realities.* New York: Praeger.

Pearce, W. B., & Littlejohn. S. (1999) *Moral conflict.* Thousand Oaks, CA: Sage.

Pearce, K. A., & Pearce, W. B. (2001). The Public Dialogue Consortium's school-wide dialogue process: A communication approach to develop citizen skills and enhance school climate. *Communication Theory, 11,* 105–123.

Pinchevski, A. (2005). *By way of interruption: Levinas and the ethics of communication.* Pittsburgh, PA: Duquesne University Press.

Roper, J., Zorn, T. E., & Weaver, C. K. (2004). *The communicative properties of science and technology dialogue: A project for the Ministry of Research, Science and Technology.* Hamilton, New Zealand: University of Waikato.

Rose, N. (1990). *Governing the soul: The shaping of the private self.* London: Routledge.

Shotter, J. (1993). *Conversational realities: The construction of life through language.* Newbury Park, CA: Sage.

Shotter, J., & Gergen, K. (1994). Social construction: Knowledge, self, others, and continuing the conversation. In S. Deetz (Ed.), *Communication yearbook 17* (pp. 3–33). Thousand Oaks, CA: Sage.

Thackaberry, J. A. (2004). Discursive opening and closing in organizational self study: Culture as the culprit for safety problems in wildland firefighting. *Management Communication Quarterly, 17,* 319–359.

Varey, R. (2002). Requisite communication for positive involvement and participation: A critical communication theory perspective. *International Journal of Applied Human Resource Management, 3:* 20–35.

Weedon, C. (1997). *Feminist practice and poststructuralist theory* (2nd ed.). Oxford: Blackwell.

White, J. B. (1983). *When words lose their meaning: Constitutions and reconstitutions of language, character and community.* Chicago: University of Chicago Press.

Young, I. (1996). Communication and the other: Beyond deliberative democracy. In S. Benhabib (Ed.), *Democracy and difference: Contesting the boundaries of the political* (pp. 120–136). Princeton, NJ: Princeton University Press.

SUGGESTED READINGS

Philosophy

Habermas, J. (1984). *The theory of communicative action*: Vol. 1. *Reason and the rationalization of society* (Trans. T. McCarthy). Boston: Beacon Press.

Weedon, C. (1997). *Feminist practice and poststructuralist theory* (2nd ed.). Oxford: Blackwell.

Theory

Ashcraft, K. L., & Mumby, D. K. (2004). *Reworking gender: A feminist communicology of organization.* Thousand Oaks, CA: Sage.

Deetz, S. (1992). *Democracy in an age of corporate colonization: Developments in communication and the politics of everyday life.* Albany, NY: State University of New York Press.

Gergen, K. J. (1994). *Realities and relationships.* Cambridge, MA: Harvard University Press.

Grossberg, L. (1997). Cultural Studies, what's in a name? In L. Grossberg. *Bringing it all back home: Essays on cultural studies.* Durham, NC: Duke University Press.

Pearce, W. B., & Cronen, V. E. (1980). *Communication, action and meaning: The creation of social realities.* New York: Praeger.

Shotter, J. (1993). *Conversational realities: The construction of life through language.* Newbury Park, CA: Sage.

Methodology

Alvesson, M., & Deetz, S. (2000). *Doing critical management research.* London: Sage.

Flyvbjerg, B. (2001). *Making social science matter.* Cambridge: Cambridge University Press.

Jagger, A. (Ed.). (2007). *Just methods: An interdisciplinary reader.* Boulder, CO: Paradigm Publishers.

Slack, J. D. (1996). The theory and method of articulation in cultural studies. In D. Morley, & K-H. Chen (Eds.), *Stuart Hall: Critical dialogues in cultural studies.* London: Routledge.

Applications

Dempsey, S. (2007). Negotiating accountability within international contexts: The role of bounded voice. *Communication Monographs, 74,* 311–332.

Holmer-Nadesan, M. (1997). Constructing paper dolls: The discourse of personality testing in organizational practice. *Communication Theory, 7,* 189–218.

Hosking D. M., Dachler, H. P., & Gergen, K. J. (Eds.). (1995). *Management and organization: Relational alternatives to individualism.* Aldershot: Avebury.

Jackson, M. H., Poole, M. S., & Kuhn, T. (2002). The social construction of technology in studies of the workplace. In L. Lievrouw, & S. Livingstone (Eds.), *Handbook of new media: Social shaping and consequences of ICTs* (pp. 236–253). London: Sage.

Kuhn, T. (2005). Engaging networks of practice through a communicative theory of the firm. In J. L. Simpson, & P. Shockley-Zalabak (Eds.), *Engaging communication, transforming organizations: Scholarship of engagement in action* (pp. 45–66). Cresskill, NJ: Hampton Press.

Pearce, K. A., & Pearce, W. B. (2001). The Public Dialogue Consortium's school-wide dialogue process: A communication approach to develop citizen skills and enhance school climate. *Communication Theory, 11,* 105–123.

Thackaberry, J. A. (2004). Discursive opening and closing in organizational self study: Culture as the culprit for safety problems in wildland firefighting. *Management Communication Quarterly, 17,* 319–359.

4

THE PROMISE OF COMMUNICATION IN LARGE-SCALE, COMMUNITY-BASED RESEARCH

Michael L. Hecht

Discussing the distinctive promise of communication is akin to explaining what we do to the naïve listener at a party. In many ways, what we study is nebulous and refining it into a short statement has always been a challenge. Thus, the task presented to us, explicating what is unique about communication, is approached with some degree of trepidation.

I start with some assumptions to limit the scope of this discourse. First, I approach communication as an interdisciplinary enterprise, defining its study broadly. If we were to restrict our discussion to those within the disciplinary boundaries of the National or International Communication Associations, I would have less to say and the substance would be less interesting. Many of the most promising communication ideas come from outside communication as a discipline (e.g., Ajzen, Bierman, Cialdini, Greenberg, Fishbein, Kreuter, Spoth, Strecher).

Second, to make this chapter manageable and differentiate it from some of the other contributors, I restrict it to the role communication can play in large-scale, community-based research. This style of research focuses on social problems in our communities (e.g., improving health and/or education) and utilizes powerful, large-sample designs to address them. I adopt this perspective not only as a means of delineating the topic, but also because I believe that this context or framework for research provides a more powerful venue for developing and testing theory as well as establishing a "communication voice" in the larger research community. While I will return to this point in the conclusion, I believe that large-scale, community-based research that addresses important social issues challenges theory and method in ways that laboratory-based research with college student samples does not and, further, that these challenges result in advances that less ambitious research agendas do not. Theories are truly valuable when they can produce change in health practices, voting patterns, and other social behaviors, rather than merely induce 18-year-old college students to provide hypothetical support for some proposition (e.g., how they would treat their dating partner or choose someone to survive in a lifeboat). Our use of communication theories and concepts to address serious social issues is not only an end in itself but also provides us with a forum that speaks to academia as well as society. Without this voice we are merely speaking to each other within a relatively small and inconsequential discipline. Those who complain that other disciplines do not pay attention to us often are cast into this position by the nature of their work rather than some failing of the academy or larger society. Many communication scholars are widely cited, but usually for work that addresses serious social issues and is conducted in an inter-disciplinary framework.

As I peruse the social scientific, large-scale, community-based research, certain trends emerge that privilege communication. In my role as a policy research reviewer for the Robert Woods Johnson Foundation, a standing member and now chairperson of a National Institute of Health review group focusing on Community-Level Health Promotion, and a NIH-funded researcher since the late 1980s, I believe that communication provides a distinctive vantage point from which to address social issues through large-scale, community-based research. Our work on message design, culture, and qualitative methodology are but three of these advantages, albeit important ones.

MESSAGE DESIGN

Communication scholars focus on the message, itself, while others see communication in a more simplistic way as a means toward an end such as health promotion. This plays out most clearly in public health campaigns. My colleague, Roxanne Parrott (2004), has long made the claim, supported by my observations as a grant reviewer, that researchers without a communication perspective rely on "informa-tion" to induce change. Lacking a deep understanding of messages, they pay little attention to what form the message takes and how it is delivered. The insufficiency of this approach is evident in a number of domains. A series of meta-analyses in school-based drug prevention, for example, demonstrates that information-only campaigns fail to influence adolescence substance use and this finding has led prevention researchers to focus on the social processes involved in these health behaviors (Tobler et al., 2000). The fact that a number of very effective prevention programs now exist across health domains reflects the emergence of a deeper understanding of communication processes (Bierman & Greenberg, 1996; Botvin, Schinke, Epstein, Diaz, & Botvin, 1995; Buller, 2006; Hawkins & Catalano, 1992; Hecht & Miller-Day, in press; Spoth, Redmond, & Shin, 2000).

Communication has much to contribute to this emerging body of knowledge. Building on rhetorical traditions while breaking away from its restrictive humanistic lens, communication scholars have long studied the forms of the message and the processes of their delivery. From McCroskey's (1968) early work on evidence and credibility, Ev Rogers' (2003; Singhal & Rogers, 2003) work on diffusion of innovation, and DeVito's work on language (1970) to more recent advances such as M. Burgoon's work on message intensity (Hamilton, Hunter, & Burgoon, 1990) and Donohue, Palmgreen and the Kentucky group's message sensation value (Donohew, Palmgreen, Zimmerman, Harrington, & Lane, 2003), this work shows that "providing" information is very much about the form of the message and how it is delivered. One can focus on any number of lines of research in this area, including work in message design (Ajzen, 2002; Fishbein & Ajzen, 1981; Parrott, 2004), message adaptation processes (Gallois, Ogay, & Giles, 2005), as well as message targeting and tailoring (Kreuter, Lukwago, Bucholtz, Clark, & Sanders-Thompson, 2003; Kreuter, Strecher, & Glasman, 1999; Strecher, Wang, Derry, Wildenhaus, & Johnson, 2002; Strecher et al., 2005). Advances in the understanding of influence processes (Cialdini, Reno, & Kallgren, 1990; Prochaska, DiClemente, & Norcross, 1992) have also contributed in this area. Thus, we can see that communication scholars have made many valuable contributions to community-based research.

While numerous message forms provide communication research with a unique perspective on public health research, prominent among these has been our understanding of the role of narrative. From the work of Walter Fisher (1987) to more recent advances from my colleague Michelle Miller-Day (2004), narrative is seen as a message structure (i.e., putting messages in the form of a story) as well as a form of persuasive appeal or argument (i.e., narrative appeals). Narrative theory conceptualizes human thought and behavior as based on story telling. Narrative form is a pervasive mode of discourse through which people organize information and experiences of the world (White, 1981). Not only are they one of the primary means for making sense of experience and moral choices (Cook-Gumperz, 1993; Fisher, 1987), but narratives also serve as an organizing principle for behavior (Botvin et al., 1995; Howard, 1991). As McAdams (1993, p. 11) notes, "We each seek to provide our scattered and often confused experiences with a sense of coherence by arranging the episodes of our lives into stories." More than thought, narratives are a meaningful form of communicative behavior through which people express themselves while planning and understanding their own actions. "Much of what passes for everyday conversation among people is storytelling of one form or another" (McAdams, 1993, p. 28). Fisher (1987) identifies narrative fidelity and narrative coherence as the basis for determining the quality of a story. Fidelity is the criterion of fit—does the story make sense to people, providing a match to their experiences? Coherence is the criterion of form—does the story hold together? These constructs also help us understand how narratives communicate and influence, guiding our development of our prevention curriculum. There are numerous examples of the role of narratives in health promotion. They have been used to promote cancer prevention and screening behaviors among Latinos/as (Larkey, Hecht, Miller, & Alatorre, 2001), lower risk behaviors in community HIV prevention programs (Fishbein & Yzer, 2003; Vaughan, Rogers, Singhal, & Swalehe, 2000), and reproductive health (Davenport-Sypher, McKinley, Ventsam, & Valdeavellano, 2002). A meta-analysis demonstrates the power of this message form (Allen et al., 2000).

Michelle Miller-Day and I grounded our line of community-based research on this narrative perspective, providing a first-hand illustration of the distinctiveness of this approach to messages. We began by studying adolescent narratives to describe the social processes of drug use and then utilized the narratives as form and content for our school-based intervention that has been selected as a federally-recognized evidence-based program (Hecht & Miller-Day, in press; Miller, Alberts, Hecht, Krizek, & Trost, 2000).[1] These stories not only convey how to resist peer influence, but, it seems, also communicate a norm of refusal and weaken belief in the positive outcomes of substance use. There is a cultural element to narratives. Narratives are intimately tied to membership in speech communities. Storytelling draws upon socially shared symbol systems which express membership while making stories meaningful to listeners. These narratives provide "good reasons" which justify actions based on the dominant stories within the group (Fisher, 1987). There is ample evidence to suggest that narratives are structured differently in various ethnic groups (Holland & Kilpatrick, 1993; Howard, 1991) and that those differences are reflected, for example, in the oral narratives in African American and Mexican American communities (Botvin et al., 1995; Kochman, 1981; Smitherman, 1977). In fact, all communication may be said to have a cultural element. Building on this understanding of culture is the second unique feature of communication I wish to highlight.

CULTURE AND COMMUNICATION

I start with the assumption that communication and culture are inseparably intertwined somewhat like the layers of a holographic image. It is hard to imagine how they might be separated, because communication is the fabric of culture and culture is the inevitable context and content of communication. A colleague, Amira de la Garza, goes so far as to suggest that communication and culture is a redundant phrase because each *is* the other.

The importance of culture as a theoretical and practical construct is reinforced in a variety of ways. Recently John Baldwin, Sandra Faulkner, Sheryl Lindsley, and I published a book that compiled 300 definitions of culture (Baldwin, Faulkner, Hecht, & Lindsley, 2006). The book identifies seven primary ways of defining culture—culture as process, function, structure, group membership, power/ideology, product, and refinement—as well as several models of these elements, all of which implicate communication.

Culture also is reflected in National Institute of Health-funded research. Its centrality is such that researchers are required to comment on ethnic, gender, and age representation in the human subjects section of all proposals. Researchers who do not represent a range of groups must justify this, a practice in direct contrast to those in our discipline (a topic I will return to in the next section). It is a topoi that culture and health, like culture and communication, are inseparable and that local or indigenous health practices must be considered in health campaigns (Dutta-Bergman, 2005; Hecht & Krieger, 2006). The mere fact that the body of knowledge and practice includes the descriptor, "community-based research," is indicative of the centrality of culture without which there can be no community.

While no discipline can claim ownership of "culture," I believe that many communication scholars advance a more sophisticated under-standing of culture that advantages them in their large-scale, community-based research. While some, whom I will call cultural generalists, treat social behavior as culture free (i.e., assume that studies of one group, usually mainstream U.S. culture, generalize to other groups unless shown otherwise), and others treat culture as a categorical variable, typically national or "racial" groupings. Communication scholars such as Philipsen, Carbaugh, De la Garza, Dutta-Bergman, Gudykunst, Giles, Jackson, Kreuter, Orbe, Ting-Toomey, and many others (with apologies to those unnamed) proffer a much more nuanced view. These take four primary approaches: cultural communication, intergroup communication, the dimensional approach, and message targeting and tailoring.

Cultural Communication

From the "cultural communication" perspective (also called ethnography of speaking), we see culture as an enactment and sense of membership (Carbaugh, 1988, 1990; Philipsen, 1992). The approach is characterized by the use of thick, ethnographic description to describe a community's socially constructed patterns of symbols, meanings, and rules and to identify cultural codes of speaking. The focus on how these codes are used to construct everyday behaviors as well as to construct membership and personhood enables us to look beyond cultural categories to see culture in daily life and provides at least four important ways of understanding culture in community-based research. To illustrate these I will use the example of utilizing culture in the construction of health messages. First, health messages must address everyday practices rather then merely broad culture images. Second, the messages must address the needs and identities of communities that are not defined only by national or "racial" borders but by neighborhoods, occupations, and social groupings as well. Third, the messages must consider the taken-for-granted rules and meanings of a people that underlie health behaviors. Finally, on the pragmatic level, cultural communication provides a guide to conducting the "community-based research methods" (Schensul et al., 2006) that dominate this branch of research. In these ways the cultural communication view adds immeasurably to our ability to conduct community-based research.

Intergroup Communication

A second branch of communication research that informs our understanding of culture is derived from the social identity theory (Tajfel and Turner, 1986) and is called the intergroup communication perspective. Most commonly identified with the work of Giles and colleagues, in some ways this perspective substitutes the construct of group membership for culture (Harwood & Giles, 2005). In other words, membership in a group, with its attendant language practices and identities, is the key organizing construct. Communication accommodation theory (CAT) (Gallois, Ogay, & Giles, 2005) is one manifestation of this approach. CAT, as it has come to be known, focuses on the adaptive processes of intergroup interaction thereby avoiding the assumption of a static state of difference. By centering the "group," like the cultural communication approach, the intergroup approach also expands the reach of culture to entities not previously considered, such as age cohorts (Williams & Nussbaum, 2001) and disability status (Ryan, Bajorek, Beaman, & Anas, 2005). The emphasis on identity was one of the influences on my own line of research on ethnic identity, including my communication theory of identity (CTI) (e.g., Hecht, Jackson, & Ribeau, 2003). Like other approaches to identity that stress its social nature, CTI is useful in examining the social aspects of health (e.g., drug-resistance strategies). The intergroup approach is particularly noteworthy when applied to health (e.g., the medical community; the older adult population) because it allows us to recognize the needs of groups that are typically under-served.

The Dimensional Approach

Next, there is a third branch, loosely allied with the intergroup approach that takes a dimensional approach to culture. Most closely associated with my deceased former colleague, Bill Gudykunst (2004), research in this tradition argues that the practices of particular groups are of less interest than those of types of groups. Borrowing from Hofstede's dimensions (2001), particular attention is paid to individualism and collectivism. Responding to criticisms of applying cultural-level constructs to the individual and dyad, later research added the "self-construal" construct, which can be seen as an individual level of individualism and collectivism, although not without serious measurement problems. This multi-level analysis provides us with the means to present culture as a society, dyadic, and interpersonal construct.

Targeting and Tailoring

Finally, at least for this review, is the role of culture in message targeting (i.e., communication to a group based on common characteristics) and tailoring (i.e., communication to an individual based on her/his characteristics) (Kreuter et al, 1999). Health research demonstrates that generic messages, those that cut across groups, are less effective than those that take into account the characteristics of the audience (Botvin et al., 1995; Hecht & Krieger, 2006; Hecht & Miller-Day, in press; Resnicow, Baronowski, Ahluwalia, & Braithwaite, 1999). This basic premise can be traced to audience analysis research but is more fully developed in marketing research; however, it is one that commonly escapes the cultural generalists. Research has demonstrated the effectiveness of these approaches, including the development of algorithms that utilize data to tailor individualized interventions (Kreuter et al., 1999; Strecher et al., 2005; Sorenson et al., 2007). Although there are numerous dimensions on which messages can be targeted or tailored (e.g., psychographics), culture, or at least group membership and identity, plays a prominent role. In addition to the obvious choices of ethnicity and gender, cultural work in this area provides a more advanced metric that includes age, socio-economics, region (e.g., rural/urban or area within a country), religion, etc. Tailoring also utilizes a host of individual variables that, at first glance, seem devoid of cultural influence. Nevertheless, many of these are derived from social identities, a construct that was liberated from the individualistic strictures of "self-concept" and made more useful in health message design. This approach to message targeting and tailoring can be loosely grouped into methods of cultural sensitivity, appropriateness, and/or grounding (Hecht & Krieger, 2006; Kreuter et al., 2003) that emerged in the health literature to guide these processes. These approaches identify a range or level of adaptation, from surface use of visual images (e.g., Latino mothers in a kitchen) to more implicit and deep cultural structures and values (e.g., use of cultural narratives).

What should be clear in these discussions of messages and culture is that a communication perspective informs methodological choices. In the next section, these methods are discussed more directly.

METHODS

As message design and culture represent conceptual contributions, communication research also makes methodological contributions. In general, public health researchers lead the way in quantitative methods. Advances such as multi-level modeling and longitudinal analyses such as growth modeling were common in health research prior to their emergence in communication research. Recent advances such as latent class analysis (Lanza, Flaherty, & Collins, 2003; Loken, 2004), latent profile analysis (DiStefano & Kamphaus, 2006), and latent transition analysis (Chung, Park, & Lanza, 2005; Graham, Collins, Wugalter, Chung, & Hansen, 1991) along with the use of missing data designs (Schafer & Graham, 2002) are emerging in the public health arena. Nevertheless, communication has a long tradition of qualitative methods, which uniquely situates the field.

Although one often hears that qualitative methods are disadvantaged in seeking the funding needed to carry out large-scale, community-based projects, this generalization tells only part of the story. First, it is clear that qualitative methods are needed in the formative stage of health message design. One-on-one and focus group interviews are common methods of developing and pilot testing messages. The use of narrative interviews (Young & Rodriguez, 2006) is particularly appealing. Second, communication plays a key role in the design and execution of community-based research in which the researcher and community are seen as co-researchers (see, for example, Schensul et al., 2006; Spoth, Greenberg, Bierman, & Redmond, 2004). As someone whose teams have recruited large samples for prevention studies, including as many as 46 schools, and participated in citywide health initiatives, it is clear that the ability to communicate is central to this emerging trend in the conduct of research. Finally, there is no denying that qualitative researchers face a challenge in arguing their methods in order to obtain the resources needed to conduct large-scale projects. However, some, like Jean Schensul of the Institute of Community Research at the University of Hartford, have shown that this is not insurmountable.

BARRIERS

With the tremendous promise exhibited in this and companion chapters one might expect the communication *discipline* to play a more prominent role in large-scale, community-based research. The centrality of communication to health theory, research, and practice would lead one to believe that many members of NCA and ICA would appear among the lists of National Institute of Health-funded researchers, interdisciplinary health publications and exemplary interventions (e.g., National Registry of Effective Prevention Programs). However, there are a number of factors holding the discipline back from fulfilling this promise; thus, I will end this chapter with a discussion of three of these barriers.

Lack of a Grant Culture

The communication discipline lacks a grant culture. Grants are not an end in and of themselves, but are typically necessary to support the type of research being discussed in this chapter (Hecht & Parrott, 2002). This may look like a trivial or at least an easily surmountable barrier, given the talent level of communication scholars. However, this is a more difficult challenge than appears on the surface. I contend that our basic disciplinary values are inconsistent with the social sciences in general and this plays out in a lack of recognition for large-scale, community-based research. This is reflected in a number of ways. For example, examine the list of distinguished NCA scholars and note how few of them have ever conducted this type of research. Next, examine our journals and see how few of research projects reported in our publications conduct this type of research through external funding. In 2006, for example, 13% of the articles published in *Communication Monographs* and *Human Communication Research* were grant supported. This has a significant impact on our graduate training, department culture, and research community.

Graduate Training Without a grant culture, our graduate students are not trained in grant writing or even thinking in terms of large-scale projects. This type of research is an acquired skill and training in our field typically offers little outside of individual research teams. Moreover, our field's belief in its own research skills causes many of us to misunderstand the methodological requirements of this type of research and the qualifications of methodologists whom funding agencies will trust with the large sums needed to support this work. Finally, our emphasis on classroom-based graduate education is at odds with the project-based learning promoted by large-scale, community-based research. The lack of post-doctoral positions in communication reflects this orientation.

Department Cultures The research cultures in our departments make large-scale, community-based research harder to conduct. The longer time frame needed for this work is not rewarded by most departments. Faculty who publish numerous, small-scale studies of the kind commonly found in *Communication Monographs* and *Human Communication Research* often are privileged over those who publish community-based work in *Health Communication* and interdisciplinary health journals. Departmental procedures for assigning research assistants that do not recognize the needs of large projects are another issue. A number of years ago Roxanne Parrott and I addressed many of these issues in an article in the *Journal of Applied Communication Research* (Hecht & Parrott, 2002); however, this was a difficult discussion even within our own department in which seven of the faculty were involved in funded research.

Research Community I believe that the communication research community's values are inconsistent with those of large-scale, community-based research. This is illustrated in a number of ways perhaps best exemplified by a recent issue of *Human Communication Research* (volume 33, number 2, April 2007) in which a series of articles were published that address social concerns. There are many qualities to like about these studies. They may well represent some of the very best research in our field. At the same time, they illustrate the points being made about our research culture. Consistent with the trends noted above, only one of these articles was supported by external funding. This, in itself, is not a problem; however, it correlates highly with other trends. First, *all* of the studies were conducted on student samples. Although college students are appropriate for some studies, it is certainly remarkable that every study in this issue was conducted in this setting. Moreover, *all* utilized a single university for their samples, which average only 167 participants per study. Does this reflect a bias? I can report from my experience that when submitting articles from large-scale studies, one involving over 6,000 participants in 35 middle schools, I have always received challenges related to the representativeness of my samples and this dates back to research I conducted in community contexts in the early 1980s and carried through to a recent study that sampled people attending church services.

Second, only three of the papers report on the ethnicity of its participants and these samples were predominantly white (at least 78%). As noted earlier in this chapter, NIH requires funding applications to report on ethnicity, gender, and age and to justify samples that are not inclusive. It is difficult to see how a predominantly white sample could be justified for any of these studies. This trend also reflects the "culture general" position discussed earlier in which research conducted on white samples is assumed to generalize. Those of us who study ethnicity are constantly asked by journal reviewers to justify non-white samples (or told to publish in intercultural journals). These demands are not typically made of studies utilizing mostly white samples. The failure to understand the role that culture plays in communication is reflected in the predominance of both the college context (e.g., age and developmental issues) as well as white samples. Attempts to change this culture (e.g., Wood and Duck, 1995) have not been successful.

Third, laboratory methods were conducted in four of the papers (with two papers reporting two small studies each), and the papers utilizing questionnaires did not report the context in which they were completed. From my experience as a grant reviewer, I can report that laboratory methods are very difficult to justify for the study of social problems. Yet, our discipline's research culture values small college student sample studies conducted in a laboratory over field-based research. Even our most basic textbooks teach that communication is contextual and yet we seem to believe unproblematically that behavior in a laboratory generalizes to other settings. While this may be the case for some behaviors, when combined with the developmental and cognitive limitations of college samples of mostly white students, one has to question the generalizability of findings largely derived from this body of research.

Finally, none of the studies utilizes any measure of behavior as an outcome and all involve a single point in time measurement. One paper utilized a physiological outcome that is appropriate, but the others rely on attitudes, intentions, and perceptions as the outcome variables. Recently, I heard a speaker refer to these as "behaviors," although clearly they are not. Moreover, the use of single point in time data limits our ability to establish causality as well as significance (i.e., do the findings hold up over time?), especially in questionnaire designs. In sum, the preference for small college sample, laboratory-based, single-point-in-time research is simply inconsistent with the values that support large-scale, community-based research that is funded by external grants.

Lack of Focus

I believe that the discipline lacks focus and this inhibits large-scale, community-based research. Many, perhaps most communication departments still are oriented toward and organized around their undergraduate curriculum that emphasizes breadth of course coverage rather than the research specialties. This has a number of implications. First, it leads to an under-emphasis on social science research methodology, with few departments willing to devote resources to even one methods specialist let alone the multiple methodologists, including statisticians, found in the best science departments doing large-scale community-based research. In addition, the difficulty in staffing multiple sections of culture and health classes at the undergraduate level inhibits the size of those areas compared to organizational communication and other areas popular with our undergraduates. Finally, the need to spread coverage inhibits the growth of a core faculty in research specialties. While breadth of coverage serves the undergraduate needs, an important function of our departments, specialization with multiple faculty within areas is needed for a research focus. While not popular, the use of non-tenure track faculty for undergraduate teaching may facilitate the growth of research specialties.

The ongoing presence of a large contingent of humanities faculty (e.g., rhetoric, performance studies) also reflects this undergraduate focus in my opinion. Departments attempting to cover both social science and humanities rarely marshal the resources needed to excel in social scientific inquiry and graduate training. Thus, attempting to do both almost inevitably dooms the social sciences to a second-class status among the social science disciplines of psychology, sociology, family studies, anthropology, etc. because the faculty must be split between the two approaches and there is rarely any synergy across these divergent approaches.

Low Aspirations

Finally, I believe that the discipline, in general, has low aspirations. This view pervades so many aspects of our disciplinary existence that it is often difficult to recognize. For example, what size do we want our departments to be? Many are thrilled with departments if they total 20 faculty members, even if they are spread across the social sciences and humanities. How does this compare to major psychology and sociology departments? Can you imagine having 20 sociologists at a major department, let alone the 8–10 communication social scientists we often find in our doctoral granting institutions? Why are we satisfied with a single laboratory for the entire department when psychologists often have individual laboratories and sociology departments sometimes house major research centers? Now extend this to staffing, faculty–student ratios, size of graduate programs (particularly when spread across humanities and social sciences), as well as other resources, and you get a picture of a discipline whose departments compare themselves to what they were like in the "bad old days" rather than to other successful departments at their university.

CONCLUSION

These are but some of the obstacles I see that inhibit actualizing our distinctiveness and building upon the advantages documented in this and other chapters throughout this book. Will the discipline change and grow? This is a difficult question to answer. When I first became department head, I was struck with a paper Jesse Delia wrote in the *Journal of the Association for Communication Administration* (1999) describing his philosophy in building the Illinois program. Jesse argued that we could fight the prevailing value systems at our institutions but we would not win because these values were held by intelligent people who, collectively, have more power than us. Applying this to the current situation, I would argue that the following steps are needed. First we need to change current thinking that is counter to the NIH mindset that values large-scale, community-based research. It will be difficult to overcome our training that emphasizes articulating "new theories" that are often constructs/hypothesitos,[2] literature reviews that are required to cover everything, research reports of multiple small studies, etc., and start to develop the methodological competencies that are needed for large sample work. We will have to change how we treat "applied" research. Testing theory through application *is* theoretical research. Currently, manuscripts dealing with social problems that are submitted to national journals may be considered too applied even if they involve theory testing and/or development. The discipline would have to come to value larger samples, longitudinal research, and a focus on social problems that mean something in society. We also need to stop seeing grants for the money they bring in rather than for the research they entail. NIH grant reviews are more scientifically rigorous than any journal review. Overall, we need to begin to value our distinctiveness in message design, the understanding of culture, and the use of qualitative methods. The immensity of this task has led some of us to veer away from the communication discipline as our source of knowledge and comparison toward the larger arena of public health or out of the academy. Yet, the promise of communication research keeps others connected.

NOTES

1. Botvin and colleagues (1995) have had similar success utilizing narrative in prevention research.
2. I thank Ken Sereno for this concept, denoting theories that are really just hypotheses. I leave the identification of these hypothesitos to the reader's imagination.

REFERENCES

Allen, M., Bruflat, R., Fucilla, R., Kramer, M., McKellips, S., Ryan, D. J., & Spieglehoff, M. (2000). Testing the persuasiveness of evidence: Combining narrative and statistical forms. *Communication Research Reports, 17,* 331–336.

Ajzen, I. (2002). Perceived behavioral control, self-efficacy, locus of control, and the theory of planned behavior. *Journal of Applied Social Psychology, 32,* 1–20.

Baldwin, J. R., Faulkner, S. L., Hecht, M. L., & Lindsley, S. L. (Eds.). (2006). *Redefining culture: Perspectives across the disciplines.* Mahwah, NJ: Lawrence Erlbaum Associates, Inc.

Bierman, K. L., Greenberg, M. T. & the Conduct Problems Prevention Research

Group. (1996). Social skill training in the FAST Track program. In R. D. Peters, & R. J. McMahon (Eds.), Preventing childhood disorders, substance abuse, and delinquency (pp. 65–89). Newbury Park, CA: Sage.

Botvin, G. J., Schinke, S. P., Epstein, J. A., Diaz, T. & Botvin, E. M. (1995). Effectiveness of culturally focused and generic skills training approaches to alcohol and drug abuse prevention among minority adolescents: Two-year follow-up results. *Psychology of Addictive Behaviors, 9*, 183–194.

Buller, D. B. (2006). Interventions to modify skin cancer related behaviors. In S. M. Miller, D. J. Bowen, R. T. Croyle, & J. H. Rowland (Eds.), *Handbook of behavioral science and cancer.* Washington, DC: APA.

Carbaugh, D. (1988). Comments of "culture" in communication inquiry. *Communication Reports, 1*, 38–41.

Carbaugh, D. (Ed.). (1990). *Cultural communication and intercultural contact.* Hillsdale, NJ: Lawrence Erlbaum.

Chung, H., Park, Y-S., & Lanza, S. T. (2005). Latent transition analysis with covariates: Pubertal timing and substance use behaviours in adolescent females. *Statistics in Medicine, 24*, 2895–2910.

Cialdini, R. B., Reno, R. R., & Kallgren, C. A. (1990). A focus theory of normative conduct: Recycling the concept of norms to reduce littering in public places. *Journal of Personality and Social Psychology, 58*, 1015–1026.

Cook-Gumperz, J. (1993). The relevant text: Narrative, storytelling, and children's understanding of genre: Response to Egan. *Linguistics and Education, 5*, 149–156.

Davenport-Sypher, B., McKinley, M., Ventsam, S., & Valdeavellano, E. E. (2002). Fostering reproductive health through entertainment-education in the Peruvian Amazon: The social construction of Bienvenida Salud. *Communication Theory, 12*, 192–205.

Delia, J. G. (1999). Building excellence in communication studies: Illinois speech communication 1975–1995 as exemplar. *JACA: Journal of the Association for Communication Administration, 28*(3), 124–131.

DeVito, J.A. (1970). *The psychology of speech and language.* New York: Random House.

Di Stefano, C., & Kamphaus, R. W. (2006). Investigating subtypes of child development: A comparison of cluster analysis and latent cluster analysis in typology creation. *Educational and Psychological Measurement, 66*, 778–794.

Donohew, L., Palmgreen, P., Zimmerman, R., Harrington, N., & Lane, D. (2003). Health risk takers and prevention (pp. 165–170). In D. Romer (Ed.), *Reducing adolescent risk.* Thousand Oaks, CA: Sage.

Dutta-Bergman, M. (2005). Theory and practice in health communication campaigns: a critical interrogation. *Health Communication, 18*, 103–122.

Fishbein, M., & Ajzen, I. (1981). Attitudes and voting behaviour: An application of the theory of reasoned action. *Progress in Applied Social Psychology, 1*, 253–313.

Fishbein, M., & Yzer, M. C. (2003). Using theory to design effective health behavior interventions. *Communication Theory, 13*, 164–183.

Fisher, W. (1987). *Human communication as narration: Toward a philosophy of reason, value, and action.* Columbia, SC: University of South Carolina Press.

Gallois, C., Ogay, T., & Giles, H. (2005). Communication accommodation theory: A look back and a look ahead. In W. Gudykunst (Ed.), *Theorizing about intercultural communication* (pp. 121–148). Thousand Oaks, CA: Sage.

Graham, J. W., Collins, L. M., Wugalter, S. E., Chung, N. K., & Hansen, W. B. (1991). Modeling transitions in latent stage-sequential processes: A substance use prevention example. *Journal of Counseling and Clinical Psychology, 59*, 48–57.

Gudykunst, W. B. (2004). *Bridging differences: Effective intergroup communication* (4th ed.). Thousand Oaks, CA: Sage.

Hamilton, M. A., Hunter, J. E., & Burgoon, M. (1990). An empirical test of an axiomatic model of the relationship between language intensity and persuasion. *Journal of Language and Social Psychology, 9*, 235–255.

Harwood, J. & Giles, H. (Eds.). (2005). *Intergroup communication: Multiple perspectives.* New York: Peter Lang.

Hawkins, J. D., Catalano, R. F. & Associates. (1992). *Communities that care: Action for drug abuse prevention.* San Francisco: Jossey-Bass, Inc.

Hecht, M. L., Jackson, R. L., & Ribeau, S. (2003). *African American communication: Exploring identity and culture* (2nd ed.). Mahwah, NJ: Lawrence Erlbaum Associates, Inc.

Hecht, M. L., & Krieger, J. K. (2006). The principle of cultural grounding in school-based substance use prevention: The Drug Resistance Strategies Project. *Journal of Language and Social Psychology, 25*, 301–319.

Hecht, M. L., & Miller-Day, M. (in press). The Drug Resistance Strategies Project: A communication approach to preventing adolescent drug use. In L. Frey, & K. Cissna (Eds.), *Handbook of Applied Communication.*

Hecht, M. L., & Parrott, R. (2002). Creating a departmental culture for communication grants. *Journal of Applied Communication Research, 30*, 382–392.

Hecht, M. L., Warren, J. W., Wagstaff, D. A., & Elek, E. (in press). Substance use, resistance skills, decision making, and refusal efficacy among Mexican and Mexican American preadolescents. *Health Communication.*

Hofstede, G. (2001). *Culture's consequences* (2nd ed.). Thousand Oaks, CA: Sage.

Holland, T. P., & Kilpatrick, A. C. (1993). Using narrative techniques to enhance multicultural practice. *Journal of Social Work Education, 29*, 302–308.

Howard, G. S. (1991). Culture tales: A narrative approach to thinking, cross-cultural psychology, and psychotherapy. *American Psychologist, 46*, 187–197.

Kochman, T. C. (1981). *Black and White: Styles in conflict.* Chicago: University of Chicago Press.

Kreuter, M. W., Lukwago, S. N., Bucholtz, D. C., Clark, E. M., & Sanders-Thompson, V. (2003). Achieving cultural appropriateness in health promotion programs: Targeted and tailored approaches. *Heath Education & Behavior, 30,* 133.

Kreuter, M. W., Strecher, V. J., & Glasman, B. (1999). One size does not fit all: The case for tailoring print materials. *Annals of Behavioral Medicine, 21,* 276–83.

Lanza, S. T., Flaherty, B. P., & Collins, L. M. (2003). Latent class and latent transition analysis. In J. A. Schinka, W. F. Velicer, & I. B. Weiner (Eds.), *Handbook of psychology:* Vol. 2, *Research methods in psychology* (pp. 663–685). Hoboken, NJ: Wiley.

Larkey, L. K., Hecht, M. H., Miller, K. I., & Alatorre, C. (2001). Hispanic cultural norms for health-seeking behavior in the face of symptoms. *Health Education and Behavior, 28,* 65–80.

Loken, E. (2004). Using latent class analysis to model temperament types. *Multivariate Behavioral Research, 39,* 625–652.

McAdams, D. (1993). *Stories we live by: Personal myths and the making of the self.* New York: William Morrow.

McCroskey, J. C. (1968). *An introduction to rhetorical communication: A Western rhetorical perspective* Englewood Cliffs, NJ: Prentice-Hall.

Miller, M. A., Alberts, J. K., Hecht, M. L., Krizek, R. L., & Trost, M. (2000). *Adolescent relationships and drug abuse.* New York: Erlbaum Publications.

Miller-Day, M. (2004). *Communication among grandmothers, mothers, and adult daughters: A qualitative study of women across three generations.* Mahwah, NJ: Lawrence Erlbaum Associates, Inc.

Parrott, R. (2004). Emphasizing "communication" in health communication. *Journal of Communication, 54,* 751–787.

Philipsen, G. (1992). *Speaking culturally: Explorations in social communication.* Albany, NY: State University of New York Press.

Prochaska, J. O., DiClemente, C. C., & Norcross, J. C. (1992). In search of how people change. *American Psychologist, 47,* 1102–1114.

Resnicow, K., Baronowski, T., Ahluwalia, J. S., & Braithwaite, R. L. (1999). Cultural sensitivity in public health: Defined and demystified. *Ethnicity and Disease, 9,* 10–21.

Rogers, E. M. (2003). *Diffusion of innovation* (5th Ed.). New York: Free Press.

Ryan, E. B., Bajorek, S., Beaman, A., & Anas, A. P. (2005). "I just want you to know that 'them' is 'me' ": Intergroup perspectives on communication and disability (pp. 117–137). In J. Harwood & H. Giles (Eds.), *Intergroup communication: Multiple perspectives.* New York: Peter Lang.

Schafer, J. L. & Graham, J. W. (2002). Missing data: Our view of the state of the art. *Psychological Methods, 7,* 147–177.

Schensul, J. J., Robison, J., Reyes, C., Radda, K., Gaztambide, S., & Disch, W. (2006). Building interdisciplinary/intersectoral research partnerships for community-based mental health research with older minority adults. *American Journal of Community Psychology, 38*(1–2), 79–93.

Singhal, A., & Rogers, E. (2003). *Combating AIDS: Communication strategies in action.* New Delhi: Sage Publications.

Skara, S., & Sussman, S. (2003). A review of 25 long-term adolescent tobacco and other drug use prevention program evaluations. *Preventive Medicine, 37*, 451–474.

Smitherman, G. (1977). *Talkin and testifyin: The language of Black America.* Boston: Houghton Mifflin.

Sorensen, G., Barbeau, E. M., Stoddard, A. M., Hunt, M. K., Goldman, R., Smith, A. et al. (2007). Tools for health: the efficacy of a tailored intervention targeted for construction laborers. *Cancer Causes Control, 18*(1), 51–59.

Spoth, R., Greenberg, M., Bierman, K., & Redmond, C. (2004). PROSPER community-university partnership model for public education systems: Capacity building for evidence-based, competence-building prevention. *Prevention Science, 5*, 31–39.

Spoth, R., Redmond, C., & Shin, C. (2000). Reducing adolescents' aggressive and hostile behaviors: Randomized trial effects of a brief family intervention 4 years past baseline. *Archives of Pediatrics & Adolescent Medicine, 154*, 1248–1257.

Strecher, V. J., Marcus, A., Bishop, K., Fleisher. L., Slengle, W., Levinson, A., Fairclough, D. L. et al. (2005). A randomized controlled trial of multiple tailored messages for smoking cessation among callers to the cancer information service. *Journal of Health Communication, 10*, 105–118.

Strecher, V. J., Wang, C., Derry, H., Wildenhaus, K., & Johnson, C. (2002). Tailored interventions for multiple risk behaviors. *Health Education Research, 19*, 619–626.

Tajfel, H., & Turner, J. C. (1986). The social identity theory of intergroup relations. In S. Worchel, & W. Austin (Eds.), *The social psychology of intergroup relations* (pp. 33–47). Monterey, CA: Brooks/Cole.

Tobler, N. S., Roona, M. R., Ochshorn, P., Marshall, D. G., Streke, A. V., & Stackpole, K. M. (2000). School-based adolescent drug prevention programs: 1998 meta-analysis. *Journal of Primary Prevention, 20*, 275–336.

Vaughan, P. W., Rogers, E. M., Singhal, A., & Swalehe, R. M. (2000). Entertainment-education and HIV/AIDS prevention: a field experiment in Tanzania. *Journal of Health Communication, 5*, 81–100.

White, H. (1981). The value of narrativity in the presentation of reality. In W. J. T. Mitchell (Ed.), *On narrative.* Chicago: The University of Chicago Press.

Williams, A. & Nussbaum, J. F. (2001). *Intergenerational communication across the lifespan.* Mahwah, NJ: Erlbaum.

Wood, J. T. & Duck, S. W. (Eds.). (1995) *Understudied relationships: Off the beaten track [Understanding relationship processes 6].* Thousand Oaks, CA: Sage.

Young, A. J., & Rodriguez, K. L. (2006). The role of narrative in discussing end-of-life care: Eliciting values and goals from text, context, and subtext. *Health Communication, 19*(1), 49–59.

SUGGESTED READINGS

Philosophy

Baldwin, J. R., Faulkner, S. L., Hecht, M. L., & Lindsley, S. L. (Eds.). (2006). *Redefining culture: Perspectives across the disciplines.* Mahwah, NJ: Lawrence Erlbaum Associates, Inc.

Hecht, M. L., & Krieger, J. K. (2006). The principle of cultural grounding in school-based substance use prevention: The Drug Resistance Strategies Project. *Journal of Language and Social Psychology, 25,* 301–319.

Parrott, R. (2004). Emphasizing "communication" in health communication. *Journal of Communication, 54,* 751–787.

Theory

Carbaugh, D. (Ed.). (1990). *Cultural communication and intercultural contact.* Hillsdale, NJ: Lawrence Erlbaum.

Fisher, W. (1987). *Human communication as narration: Toward a philosophy of reason, value, and action.* Columbia, SC: University of South Carolina Press.

Harwood, J. & Giles, H. (Eds.). (2005). *Intergroup communication: Multiple perspectives.* New York: Peter Lang.

Hecht, M. L., Jackson, R. L., & Ribeau, S. (2003). *African American communication: Exploring identity and culture* (2nd ed.). Mahwah, NJ: Lawrence Erlbaum Associates, Inc.

Methodology

Lanza, S. T., Flaherty, B. P., & Collins, L. M. (2003). Latent class and latent transition analysis. In J. A. Schinka, W. F. Velicer, & I. B. Weiner (Eds.), *Handbook of psychology: Vol. 2, Research methods in psychology* (pp. 663–685). Hoboken, NJ: Wiley.

Miller-Day, M. (2004). *Communication among grandmothers, mothers, and adult daughters: A qualitative study of women across three generations.* Mahwah, NJ: Lawrence Erlbaum Associates, Inc.

Schensul, J. J., Robison, J., Reyes, C., Radda, K., Gaztambide, S., & Disch, W. (2006). Building interdisciplinary/intersectoral research partnerships for community-based mental health research with older minority adults. *American Journal of Community Psychology, 38*(1–2), 79–93.

Applications

Hecht, M. L., & Miller-Day, M. (in press). The Drug Resistance Strategies Project: A communication approach to preventing adolescent drug use. In L. Frey & K. Cissna (Eds.), *Handbook of Applied Communication.*

Hecht, M. L., & Parrott, R. (2002). Creating a departmental culture for communication grants. *Journal of Applied Communication Research, 30,* 382–392.

5

THE IMPORTANCE OF COMMUNICATION SCIENCE IN ADDRESSING CORE PROBLEMS IN PUBLIC HEALTH

Joseph N. Cappella and Robert C. Hornik

COMMUNICATION RESEARCH VERSUS COMMUNICATION SCIENCE

An all-too-common assumption among funding agencies is that communication is only a practical art and, when it is raised to a principled scientific practice, confused with the simple use of scientific research methods. Our view is that communication scholarship can be scientific and that part of our role is—through our research practices—to promote communication as a science, not just a practical art employing scientific methods.

Entire industries of journalists, public relations experts, and advertisers are engaged in communication research. This research is quantitative, qualitative, and sometimes intuitive. This industry provides important advice to its clients both for commercial and for social marketing purposes. Sometimes this advice is based on information gathered using scientific methods. However, one must not confuse scientific methods used in studying communication with the goal of developing scientific knowledge about communication (Pavitt, 2001).

Communication researchers must certainly maintain high standards in the way they deploy scientific methods but they must be engaged in and, in the process, convince external funders that their work is undertaken to advance the science of communication. Conducting research using the scientific method and conducting scientific research are two different activities which may share method and logic but not goals necessarily. Let us illustrate the point with a typical approach to the study of health messages.

Messages designed to achieve persuasive goals can be conceptualized in an infinite number of different ways. The number of different message components and their combinations that could possibly affect a message's overall effectiveness is infinite. For example, consider designing a simple brochure to be placed in a doctor's offices encouraging male patients over 40 to obtain a regular Prostate Specific Antigen (PSA) test along with a digital rectal exam. In addition to questions about the brochure's color, font, the use of pictures, reading levels, technical terms, length, and so on, the designer must decide whether to use gain or loss frames for presenting positive and negative consequences, personal stories, statistics, intense language, strong arguments and evidence, and a thousand other possible considerations. In the face of such complexity, why not simply test each message that might be used in a public health campaign, message by message, and population by population guided by intuition and past practice? Given an infinity of message features, a plausible case can be made for testing the effectiveness of each unique message in each context rather than developing theories that might provide insight across contexts. After all, if the goal is increasing the proportion of men obtaining a regular PSA test, then a brochure which does so serves the public good.[1]

The obvious counterargument is inefficiency. Individualized message testing in the absence of theory to direct the testing and in the absence of controlled testing procedures produces little knowledge that can be transferred to other contexts. The goal of theory-driven message testing is to generate knowledge that can be transferred to parallel cancer control contexts. To find that post-test intentions to get a PSA test annually are higher after reading a brochure than before provides no information about what particular feature of the brochure produced elevated intention or whether it was some particular combination of features.

Even if the testing procedure allows for isolation of the key message feature responsible for the favorable effects on intention, not knowing why the feature had its effects creates other inefficiencies that stymie the development of useful knowledge. For example, suppose two brochures are compared that differ only in the use of gain versus loss frames with the loss-framed version producing greater elevation in the intention to screen. If we also do not know why the loss frame was more effective, we are at a loss to connect findings with this message feature to other findings on different features that employ the same mechanism. So if the effects are mediated by emotional processes linked to the arousal of threat and efficacious means of alleviating that threat, then the effects of gain and loss frames might be understood as operating in a manner that is parallel to other message features that activate withdrawal emotions such as fear, anxiety, and apprehension. The results would be a much more parsimonious way to think about the very complex—indeed infinitely complex—world of message features and their effectiveness.

Theory-based scientific knowledge means generating propositions that meet ordinary definitions as scientific ones—namely that they represent causal claims that have a truth value well beyond their context and historical period of application. Such propositions answer the questions: "why and how." They do so in a way that gives us information that is much less constrained by the exigencies of historical time and immediate context.

Such knowledge claims—if we can generate them—are extremely practical. We have all heard the old adage—attributed to Kurt Lewin—that "there is nothing so practical as a good theory." Theories and theory-based knowledge are practical precisely because they establish (or at least seek to establish) knowledge claims that answer the why question by establishing plausible causal mechanisms linking concepts and doing so within and beyond contexts of immediate application.

It may appear to some that causality and mechanism—that is, the WHY of relationship between concepts—are the least practical components of research practices. Nothing can be further from the truth or from reality. Simply knowing that a particularly at-risk subpopulation prefers one communication source over another, or one newer tool to an older tool, or a message with some feature (e.g. loss frame) to one with a different feature (e.g. gain frame) is practical knowledge (and useful!). But such information is not scientific knowledge because there are an infinite number of communication sources and an infinite number of message features that exist and will exist.

If our research fails to ask and, therefore, never raises the why questions, our research will forever be behind the curve of changing communication modality and content. Now maybe this is a good business plan for us grant-getters but it is not good—nor practical—science nor efficient practice. Also claims that are not scientific ones will be inefficient ones. Also, claims that do not make mechanisms known do not tell us how to craft our interventions.

What are interventions anyway? They are ways to step in between an initial set of conditions and an outcome to alter the outcome in a desired direction. Take another message example that is receiving more and more attention in the research literature—the role of narrative forms in communicating health information (Kreuter et al., 2007). Narratives seem to be preferred by a wide range of audience members in contrast to expository forms. So narratives look like a good delivery vehicle for health information of various sorts from prevention to post-treatment life quality. So why do we need to know why they function this way?

Without knowing why, we cannot intervene in the creation of effective narratives because we don't know what it is about them that allows them to work. If we did—even if that knowledge of causal mechanism was partial—then we would have a much better idea of how to intervene in the creation of narrative-type delivery vehicles for cancer control information. So would knowledge of this kind be practical? You bet it would! What makes it practical is the knowledge of intervening mechanisms. And what kind of research is this? Is this your typical ivory-tower basic science with no window to the world? In part, yes but in a real and fundamental way this kind of basic science is very applied because it—like any good theory-based knowledge—not only gives us knowledge *that* narrative delivery vehicles work but knowledge of *how* to create future interventions with narrative that also work.

In short, theoretical knowledge must be the choice over simple message testing approaches for very practical reasons. We want our research to be efficient and so do funders. Theory-driven research about message effects allows us to isolate which message features are most responsible for the consequences of a given message and, when the mechanisms are understood as well, to connect message features that would otherwise be seen as completely disconnected as operating through the same theoretical mechanisms.

This narrow claim about message features is true more broadly as well. Scientific methods can be important ways to answer practical questions but when in service of questions—no matter how important—that are tied only to a particular time and place will necessarily be inefficient at generating theoretical knowledge claims. In turn, such approaches undersell what the field of communication can be and sometimes is—a science with the capacity to generate efficient, scientific knowledge.

QUESTIONS OF ACKNOWLEDGED
SOCIAL CONSEQUENCE

In addition to conducting research that is driven by theory, communication researchers must also be willing to engage broad questions that are acknowledged to be of core social consequence. Often this will mean studying problems that others—perhaps many others—are also studying, problems that appear to be intransigent to intervention, utterly complex, but acknowledged widely as core social problems. This claim seems to be such an obvious requirement of high quality communication science as to be unworthy of mention.

Too often established researchers and researchers-to-be turn to more tractable problems or to problems that represent their own research identities more closely rather than problems that are identified by NIH or NSF as core social and behavioral problems. For example, smoking rates in the United States have declined steadily but slowly for about four decades. Currently about 21% of the U.S. population are smokers. These may be hard core smokers whose genetic and behavioral histories make them very difficult to move from the smoker to "former smoker" category. Nevertheless, this is one of the very few behaviors known to be a cause of lung cancer and other serious diseases. Thousands of research articles have been written about the reduction of smoking and interventions aimed at increasing quitting or seeking treatment. It can be daunting for researchers—and certainly for new researchers—to find ways to contribute to the knowledge base on a problem of this complexity.

If communication researchers and the graduate students they train are going to participate in so-called "Big Science" research activities, then they will need to be willing to address questions which seem insoluble or seem at least to be intransigent to ready solution. They cannot expect funders to be excited about their own sometimes too narrow domains of interest unless they can connect to established problems of consequence.

As a practical matter, this means that researchers and the students they train must: (1) be willing to work with a wide range of other scientists in collaborative, interdisciplinary—sometimes called transdisciplinary—research projects; and (2) maintain awareness of approaching social and behavioral problems needing the attention of communication researchers. Much of the externally funded research in today's tight funding environment is transdisciplinary. Transdisciplinary research implies that the problems being addressed cannot be solved by researchers from one or another discipline but requires the simultaneous expertise of researchers from multiple disciplines. Such collaborative groups can be exciting intellectually and can create unanticipated synergies. They also offer challenges in translating ideas and methods and in achieving consensus on how best to proceed. In one of our projects funded by the National Human Genome Research Institute, the research team consists of two members from communication, one from medical genetics, a bioethicist, a behavioral genetics specialist, two lawyers, a genetics counselor, and behavioral scientist specializing in health disparities. The project is focused on ethical issues in genetics research and testing. Synergies and challenges abound!

Core social and behavioral problems are not stagnant but mutate as well as moving on and off the stage of funders' agendas. The problem of increasing childhood obesity (Kaplan, Liverman, & Kraak, 2005) has been developing in the U.S. for the past three decades and yet has reached epidemic proportions and hot white media attention only recently. In June of 2006 the FDA approved the first vaccine to reduce cervical cancer. It is 70% effective against the viruses that cause cervical cancer. The approval was heralded as having the potential to save the lives of about 4000 women every year in the United States who die from cervical cancer and much larger numbers internationally. However, resistance in some segments of the public—perhaps because the HPV virus is sexually transmitted—has stymied the widespread use of this vaccine so far. Both the childhood obesity epidemic and the HPV vaccine are health developments which pose important social issues to which communication researchers can (and have) contributed significantly. In addition to addressing core social problems which have been on the agendas of national health and science funders for many years, researchers need to be attentive to developing issues and ready to apply their scientific skills to their solution.

CORE ISSUES IN COMMUNICATION RESEARCH: REACH, EFFECTIVENESS, AND EFFICIENCY

It would be foolish to try to define or even to put boundaries on the core questions that are or could be addressed by communication researchers. The field's breadth and diversity would make any such venture doomed to failure. At the same time, the utility of communication research in social and behavioral interventions aimed at alleviating core problems will often be expected to get information to the right target audience in a form that works to achieve the desired change and to do so as inexpensively as possible. One set of useful catchwords to describe what communication science seeks to achieve in information diffusion is *reach, effectiveness,* and *efficiency.*

Reach

Information that fails to reach the target population cannot possibly affect the problem to which it is directed. Maximizing the reach of information, making it available to underserved populations and available to broader populations in the society is a minimal requirement for an effective communication intervention. Reach is often not easily achieved especially in underserved populations. In an era when the excess of information seems to be the problem not the dearth of information, reach can still pose serious difficulties for interventions. Studies of communication campaigns aimed at achieving changes in health behaviors identify failure to achieve sufficient exposure of the campaign's messages a major reason for failure (Hornik, 2002; Snyder & Hamilton, 2002). Underserved populations are often underserved in the quantity and quality of the information they need to make informed decisions about healthy life styles as well as appropriate treatment options. Communication research must be ready to offer solutions to the question of how to reach the target audience with information.

Effectiveness

Communication content can reach the target population but that is not enough; it must also be effective. Messages must contain both the needed content and form if they are to change behavior, improve decision-making, or enhance the quality of life. Communication scientists must be dedicated to studying which forms for communicating information are most effective given the target audience and desired outcome. Information needs to include arguments which are effective and information that is usable, in forms that make the content attention-getting, accessible, and credible while avoiding distraction. The messages must appeal to audiences which bring different prior experience and cultural understandings. These studies must be concerned with the best means for conveying various types of risk as well as information to build audience members' sense of personal efficacy. In short, communication science must be dedicated to understanding and designing communications that are effective in addition to their ability to reach the targeted audience.

Efficiency

Even when information reaches its target audience in an effective form, the communication intervention needs to be efficient and provide maximum impact at the lowest cost. Although the most effective intervention program might be to design for each person a personally delivered, unique diet of information pertinent to their needs, such a program is cost prohibitive and is likely to preserve the disparities that already exist between the information-rich and information-poor. Communication science needs to be exploring delivery systems for information that are efficient even in today's highly segmented, competitive media environments. New technologies can allow delivery of personally tailored information to assist in prevention (Rimer & Kreuter, 2006), decision-making about diagnosis, and survivorship. Understanding which outlets for information that people use for given problems—both people not at immediate risk and those at serious risk—allows placing targeted campaigns in the most efficient channels. Understanding the most efficient means of reaching the public with effective information ensures that even small effects will translate into substantial, cost-efficient gains for the entire population.

Not every communication study designed can address each of the issues sketched above. But our experience suggests that research undertaken to solve significant social problems in a collaborative environment looks to communication science to provide sound advice about the delivery of information. The details of the advice sought and given are often context-specific but these specifics can be viewed as answering three necessary questions: how can the information get to the right targets; how can the information be made most effective; what is the most efficient means of getting the information to the target group?

THE CENTER FOR EXCELLENCE IN CANCER COMMUNICATION (CECCR) AT PENN

For the past several years the CECCR at the Annenberg School for Communication has been funded by the National Cancer Institute to study specific problems in cancer communication. Our research has been highly collaborative, involving researchers from across the campus in disciplines as diverse as medical genetics, psychiatry, medicine, marketing, anthropology, psychophysiology, psychology, and brain science.

Our center has a unique focus dealing centrally with the effects of public information about cancer. For good or for ill, we are a society dominated by the news and entertainment media and the internet. For good or for ill, we are socialized by these media; learning a great deal from them about what is healthy and risky, what new health developments there are, and what science can tell us as well as how it can misdirect.

There is no question that health professionals play an extremely important role in providing information to their patients about risk, testing, diagnosis, treatment, and care. However, these same patients enter the medical system assuming and knowing a great deal about the processes and the disease they are facing.

The public arena of communication provides this information. The public arena must be harnessed to provide useful information, for everyone, that is effective, leading to healthier lifestyle choices, and a readiness to receive the tailored advice and information of health professionals. That is why we have chosen to focus on the role of public communication about cancer.

Three Projects

Within this broad orientation to public information and cancer, the Center's researchers are focusing on three distinct arenas of research. The first seeks to understand how people search for useful, accurate information about cancer and how this information affects decisions they make about testing, treatment, and care.

This research is undertaken in response to two developments: (1) a focus on patients as active consumers of health care information; and (2) the explosion of health information available to consumers through the internet as well as other mass media sources. If patients are invited, indeed encouraged, to be active participants in their health decisions, from which sources will their information come? How will they manage the volume, diversity, and credibility of the information available to them? Will the strategies they choose lead to better or worse decisions about health care?

The second project focuses on using mass media PSAs to motivate adult smokers to quit and to seek help in quitting. A great deal of research has been directed at designing effective mass media campaigns for adolescents to keep them from smoking and to get them to stop if they have already started. These campaigns—run at the state and national levels—have been pretty effective overall and we know a great deal about what works with adolescent audiences.

However, fairly recent data have shown that the period from 18 to 30 years is a crucial transition for adolescent smokers who will move during this period to becoming habituated smokers or giving up or being only social smokers. These groups and older adults—who are more likely to be concerned about quitting—have been understudied.

Appeals to adolescents typically involve more sensational ad formats and arguments about resisting the manipulation (and lies) of the tobacco companies. Adults have different values and will need different appeals and ad formats.

The third project is concerned with communicating about genetic risk to empower people rather than inviting feelings of fatalism. Developments in molecular genetics have been growing at a very rapid pace and will continue to do so. There is good evidence for a genetic basis for breast and prostate cancers, some types of colon cancer and for genetic variants associated with complex behavioral traits such as substance abuse. Accompanying these developments in science are two parallel developments in the public sphere: (1) very strong interest in genetics by the news media; and (2) the possibility that the public will infer incorrectly that genetic susceptibility to disease or to lifestyles means they have lost control of their lives. The consequence of these trends could be an increased sense of fatalism rather than empowerment. How can information about genetic influences on disease and behavior be presented to empower recipients and minimize their sense of fatalism?

These three projects are designed to ask questions about reach, effectiveness, and efficiency. Project one focuses on reach and efficiency of cancer information sources under different audience motivations. Projects two and three are concerned with the effectiveness of anti-smoking messages for adults and communicating genetic risk for efficacy and empowerment. What have they been finding?

Project One: Cancer Information Sources   Research in the CECCR on the way that the general and cancer population seeks (and scans for) information about cancer is primarily descriptive. It seeks to be highly precise in its descriptions of which sources of communication the population uses to obtain information and whether this information is effective in producing healthy activities, appropriate testing procedures and elevated quality of life after treatment. These data are and will be a treasure trove of information for practitioners seeking to mount campaigns and interventions with the populations of cancer victims and with general population groups. These data can direct planners toward sources that people use and don't use and hence guide the wise expenditure of funds (Niederdeppe, Hornik, & Kelly, 2007).

At the same time, the research doesn't answer the why question about information sources—why is it that that certain sources are preferred by certain subgroups? What it is about the people, the sources, their interaction, the social conditions, etc. that lead to selection and avoidance? We must begin to answer these questions because without answers—even partial ones—we cannot know anything about whether other forms of new communication will be employed or avoided in the context of cancer information seeking.

This project has produced findings that mostly comport with their *a priori* expectations—information seeking is often though not always associated with positive outcomes such as increased intake of fruits and vegetables. So information seeking is in general a good thing and should be encouraged.

However, one of the tentative results has identified a place to inquire deeply about the mechanism of information seeking—PSA testing and information seeking. Preliminary analyses have suggested that for those who engaged in information seeking in one year and who had had a prior PSA test, PSA testing in the next year is less likely. Why is this? Is it the information they encounter in the ensuing period? If so, is this outcome a benefit or cost to men? We need to know why information-seeking is functioning as it does in this context because there is either a problem to be remedied or an opportunity to be pursued.

Project Two: Anti-smoking Ads   The practical problem is increasing the likelihood that smokers will seek treatment to deal with their addiction. Message design requires focusing on both content and how the content is presented—that is, format. Much research has argued that message formats need to be harnessed to gain the audience's attention. But the other side of attention is distraction. So we have been asking how certain types of attention-getting features of video-based messages might function to gain attention or to be distracting (Lang, 2006). Our research has focused on message sensation value (12–14 specific characteristics of messages) (Morgan, Palmgreen, Stephenson, Hoyle, & Lorch, 2003) and on the presence of smoking cues in anti-smoking ads. All are potential attention-getters. However, our story to date is that—at least in adult smokers—these features might be more of a distraction than an attention-getting mechanism.

We have results from four studies so far employing primarily adult smokers and technologies that include self-report, recall, BOLD fMRI (Langleben et al., forthcoming 2008), physiological measures, and self-reported smoking urge. One of the key outcomes from dissertation work by Yahui Kang (Kang, Cappella, Strasser, & Lerman, in press) is that smokers' self-reported urge rises when they view anti-smoking ads with smoking cues in them but only if the ad's arguments against smoking are weak; these results are supported by some physiological data as well (Cacioppo, Tassinary, & Berntson, 2007). We believe that these and other findings have consequence for ad makers (Kang, Cappella, & Fishbein, 2006).

Project Three: Communicating Genetic Risk   Our content analytic work about genetic risk information is primarily a descriptive map of the news environment regarding how genetic risk is portrayed. For example, statements about genetic risk in the news tend to have a deterministic tinge to them.

In some of our studies, when people were exposed to genetic risk information, they tended to end up feeling less efficacious and at the same time more intent on acting in a healthy way especially for vulnerable groups (Cappella, Lerman, Romanton, & Baruh, 2005). When genetic risk is conceptualized as a kind of threat information, one is led to focus on the importance of efficacy information to counter the threat. Secondary focus lands on the best delivery vehicles for such information with our research now on narrative forms as a simple format to gain attention and provide modeling (Kreuter et al., 2007).

CONCLUSION

This chapter has addressed a view of what should be distinctive about communication research. The perspective revolves around three broad claims: that distinctive communication research must: (1) address core social problems about (2) the reach, effectiveness and efficiency of information pertinent to the problem (3) in a way that provides answers that meet the requirements of scientific knowledge.

These are strong demands applicable more to a research program than to each individual study conducted as a part of programmatic work. These criteria also represent aspirations that are not always met in reality. Mature scholarship deserving of resources from funds provided by the taxpayer should strive for nothing less.

NOTE

1. PSA tests are considered controversial in some medical circles (Concato et al., 2006).

REFERENCES

Cacioppo, J. T., Tassinary, L. G., & Berntson, G. G. (2007). *Psychophysiological science: Interdisciplinary approaches to classic questions about the mind.* New York: Cambridge University Press.

Cappella, J. N. (2006). Integrating message effects and behavior change theories: Organizing comments and unanswered questions. *Journal of Communication, 56,* S265–S279.

Cappella, J. N., Lerman, C., Romantan, A., & Baruh, L. (2005). News about genetics and smoking: Priming, family smoking history, and news story credibility inferring genetic susceptibility to tobacco addiction. *Communication Research, 32,* 478–502.

Concato, J., Wells, C. K., Horwitz, R. I., Penson, D., Fincke, G., Berlowitz, et al. (2006). The effectiveness of screening for prostate cancer: A nested case-control study. *Archives of Internal Medicine, 166,* 38–43.

Hornik, R. C. (2002). Public health communication: Making sense of contradictory evidence. In R. C. Hornik (Ed.), *Public health communication* (pp. 1–22). Mahwah, NJ: Erlbaum.

Kang, Y., Cappella, J. N., & Fishbein, M. (2006). The attentional mechanism of message sensation value: Interaction between message sensation value and argument quality on message effectiveness. *Communication Monographs, 73,* 351–378.

Kang, Y., Cappella, J. N., Strasser, A., & Lerman, C. (in press). The effect of smoking cues in antismoking advertisements on smoking urge and psychophysiological reactions. *Nicotine and Tobacco Research.*

Kaplan, J. P., Liverman, C. T., & Kraak, V I. (Eds.). (2005). *Preventing childhood obesity: Health in the balance.* Washington, DC: National Academies Press.

Kreuter, M. W., Green, M. C., Cappella, J. N., Slater, M. D., Wise, M. E., Storey, D., et al. (2007). Narrative communication in cancer prevention and control: A framework to guide research and application. *Annals of Behavioral Medicine, 33,* 221–235.

Lang, A. (2006). Using the limited capacity model of motivated mediated message processing to design effective cancer communication messages. *Journal of Communication, 56*(Suppl. 1), S57–S80.

Langleben, D. D., Loughead, J. W., Ruparel, K., Hakun, J. G., Busch-Winokur, S., Strasser, A. A., et al. (forthcoming). Reduced pre-frontal and temporal lobe processing and recall of high "sensation value" anti-tobacco ads. *NeuroImage.*

Morgan, S. E., Palmgreen, P., Stephenson, M. T., Hoyle, R. H., & Lorch, E. P. (2003). Associations between message features and subjective evaluations of the sensation value of antidrug public service announcements. *Journal of Communication, 53,* 512–526.

Niederdeppe, J., Hornik, R. C., & Kelly, B. J. (2007). Examining the dimensions of cancer-related information seeking and scanning behavior. *Health Communication, 22,* 153–167.

Pavitt, C. (2001). *The philosophy of science and communication theory.* Huntington, NY: Nova Science Publishers.

Rimer, B., & Kreuter, M. (2006). Advancing tailored health communication: A persuasion and message effects perspective. *Journal of Communication, 56,* s1. S184.

Snyder, L. B., & Hamilton, M. A. (2002). A meta-analysis of US health campaign effects on behavior: Emphasize enforcement, exposure, and new information and beware the secular trend. In R. C. Hornik (Ed.), *Public health communication* (pp. 357–384). Mahwah, NJ: Erlbaum.

SUGGESTED READINGS

Philosophy and Theory

Cappella, J. N. (2006). Integrating message effects and behavior change theories: Organizing comments and unanswered questions. *Journal of Communication, 56*, S265–S279.

Lang, A. (2006). Using the limited capacity model of motivated mediated message processing to design effective cancer communication messages. *Journal of Communication, 56*(Suppl 1), S57–S80.

Pavitt, C. (2001). *The philosophy of science and communication theory.* Huntington, NY: Nova Science Publishers.

Applications

Kang, Y., Cappella, J. N., & Fishbein, M. (2006). The attentional mechanism of message sensation value: Interaction between message sensation value and argument quality on message effectiveness. *Communication Monographs, 73*, 351–378.

Kang, Y., Cappella, J. N., Strasser, A., & Lerman, C. (in press). The effect of smoking cues in antismoking advertisements on smoking urge and psychophysiological reactions. *Nicotine and Tobacco Research.*

Methodology

Cacioppo, J. T., Tassinary, L. G., & Berntson, G. G. (. (2007). *Psychophysiological science: Interdisciplinary approaches to classic questions about the mind.* New York: Cambridge University Press.

Langleben, D. D., Loughead, J. W., Ruparel, K., Hakun, J. G., Busch-Winoker, S., Strasser, A.A., et al. (forthcoming). Reduced pre-frontal and temporal lobe processing and recall of high "sensation value" anti-tobacco ads. *NeuroImage.*

6

RESEARCHING CULTURE IN CONTEXTS OF SOCIAL INTERACTION
An Ethnographic Approach, a Network of Scholars, Illustrative Moves

Gerry Philipsen

In this chapter I report on an approach to the study of communication, and on the work of an interconnected group of scholars within the discipline of communication that is actively using and improving this approach in multiple contexts, languages, cultures, and arenas of practice. The approach is grounded in a simple but profound and consequential learning that, over the years, the participants in this group have achieved through their disciplined and systematic studies. That learning is that wherever and whenever there is communication, there are traces of culture laced through it. The learning began as a working assumption, adopted several decades ago (Philipsen, 1989a). Now it stands as a rich and robust finding demonstrated across the work of this group, in the past and in multiple ongoing projects. Our enterprise has been principally an academic and theoretic one. But we have also learned that these traces of culture, and the understandings we produce of them, are an important force in the lives of individuals and communities.

The chapter unfolds in three related parts. First is the approach that I and my colleagues take to the study of communication: (1) a focus on local means and meanings of communication in particular social milieus; and (2) an ethnographic method for the study of those means and meanings in any given situation. Second is the development, within the communication discipline, of a network of scholars who practice this approach and educate others to use it. The third presents two examples of how participants in this network are applying this approach to the study of cultural factors in communication in order that they might understand and shape communication in important arenas of contemporary social practice.

A CULTURALLY-ORIENTED APPROACH TO THE STUDY OF COMMUNICATION

There are two aspects to what I am describing here as an approach to the study of communication: (1) the manner; and (2) the object, of the approach. To name the manner in one word, it is ethnography, and I begin with that.

The ethnographer is concerned to approach a research site with an attitude of exploration, that is, with curiosity about what may be found there. Typically, a research site is an organization, community, neighborhood, locale, or country, that is, a physical site in which people are living and interacting, including digital locales. A site for ethnographic inquiry could also be a body of textual material that has been constructed for the purposes of research. In such cases, the materials examined could be a batch of letters, a collection of media reports, electronic recordings of life stories, or other materials that constitute a body of discourse that can be approached in an exploratory way for an ethnographic purpose.

To speak of an ethnographic purpose requires that such a purpose be defined. I treat it as such if the researcher approaches a body of materials not only in an exploratory manner but also with an eye and an ear to the discovery of local means and meanings, especially when those local means and meanings can be shown to have some history in the site in which they are experienced. To specify further, as an ethnographer of ways of communicating, the ethnographer trains her eyes and ears to local means of communicating, and to a local system of meanings associated with those means.

Given the above exposition of ethnography as exploratory inquiry into local means and meanings, and ethnography of communication as exploratory inquiry into local means and meanings of communication, a researcher could approach a neighborhood, village, organization, scene, or nation, or a corpus of letters, stories, or materials drawn from same, and if the researcher were interested in finding there evidence of local means of communication and their meanings to those who used and experienced them, that researcher would, in my definition, be an ethnographer of communication. This definition of ethnography of communication could be fully satisfied in studies of social networks, communities of practice, or communities that are linked electronically, that is, communities that are not necessarily defined by traditional notions of space.

As exploratory, curious observers, ethnographers ask, about any particular site, whether it is a neighborhood, an organization, a community, a nation, a group, a scene, or an assemblage of texts: What are the means of communication that are (or were) being deployed here? Obvious examples of such means are language varieties, dialects, ways of speaking, gestural systems, visual communication, strategic silence, communicative forms such as stories and jokes, talk, writing, graphic and other visual means, and such hybrid means as electronic mail. This enumeration of means is meant to be suggestive, not definitive. Part of the purpose of being exploratory is to find, in some site, means of communication that might not have been anticipated in some pre-formulated check-list of possible means or ways of communicating. It is to be open to discovering in any particular time or place how it is that people communicate.

The ethnographer of communication explores not only the means but also asks: What are the meanings of these means to those who use and experience them in this time and place? A given language variety, way of speaking, gestural system, font, communication technology, and the like, are always and everywhere not merely a means for conveying something about the world that is in some way separable from the means being used. It is something with a history, in the site, and with rich associations that are woven through the site's history and present activity. And it is something whose existence and use are potentially a source of identity or alienation, power or submission, pleasure or displeasure, solidarity or separation, and so forth, for those using and experiencing it. Thus, the teacher's use of one language or another; the physician's smile and eye contact with a patient or the physician's studied avoidance of such intimacies; the company presenter's use (or not) of PowerPoint; the use of a particular form of greeting or personal address over another available form; such are always potentially consequential in their own right and not just for the content that presumably their use is intended to convey, but consequential to those who use and experience them because of their significance to the parties who are involved with their use.

The ethnography of communication, as I describe it here, involves not only exploratory inquiry, *in situ*, into the means and meanings of communication, but also involves the use of specifiable investigative resources. The ethnographer draws on two types of such resources. One is various descriptive frameworks—schemes to aid observation—that have been suggested by practitioners. Chief among these is a descriptive framework first set forth by Dell Hymes in 1962 and subsequently modified by Hymes and others (Albert, 1964; Hymes, 1962, 1972). Complementary to these are frameworks developed by scholars in the communication discipline, including those by Philipsen (1987, 1992, 1997), Carbaugh, Gibson, and Milburn (1997), and Philipsen, Coutu, and Covarrubias (2005). These frameworks, schemes, and guides all have one purpose: They help an investigator discover something about the means and meanings of communication in a given case. In this regard they are a general resource for learning about something that is very particular—the means and meanings of communication in particular times and places. These schemes suggest things to notice, to look for and to listen for, and ways to record, analyze, and interpret one's findings.

Three recent examples of the type of inquiry I described above, each of which was conducted by a scholar in the communication discipline, immediately follow. The first is Michaela Winchatz's (2001) study of personal address in Germany. Winchatz, an American who is fluent in German, has over several years examined a broad array of communicative phenomena in Germany, always working in the German language. For one study, she spent ten months observing daily life and conducting fifty research interviews with the purpose of examining how Germans address each other orally, with special attention to the use of the German second person pronoun forms *du* ("you" in English) and *Sie* (also "you" in English). *Du* is generally considered a more informal way to address someone as the English "you" and *Sie* a more formal way to do the same thing. In her work on forms of personal address in German everyday interaction, Winchatz was concerned, first, to document patterns of usage and, second, to discover the significance of the use of these two forms to the Germans who used and experienced them.

In the following brief excerpt from Winchatz's first published report of her fieldwork we are given some idea as to how an exploratory researcher of the means and meanings of communication, in a particular site, might work, at the levels of description and interpretation. She reports a comment by Johann, a 57-year-old man who is a high school teacher in Germany and who, during his years in the classroom addressed his students with the informal *du*. Walking to the store one day with Johann, Winchatz observed him greet a former student and in so doing addressed her with the formal *Sie*. Later, he commented to

Winchatz that "With this [use of *Sie*] I recognize that they are no longer my students, they are adults" (Winchatz, 2001: 347). Johann's conduct and his explanation of it to Winchatz provide several points of data that a fieldworker can use to construct an account of: (1) a means of communication (the use of *du* and *Sie* as forms of personal address); and of (2) the rich meanings that the use of such forms can have for people. For example, Johann's retrospective explanation provides possible insights as to the significance, to him, in one situation, of using the *Sie* form. *Sie* here is, he says, a resource through which he accomplishes something ("with this I recognize"), that something being his acknowledgement of his interlocutor's status now as an "adult." This one datum suggests one sense of one aspect of the meaning potential of one communicative form. Over a year of fieldwork, Winchatz assembled hundreds of such data points, and in her reports of her findings she presents a systematic and complex synthesis and interpretation of the contemporary German system of practices and meanings with regard to pronominal personal address, the thoroughness and richness of which are only hinted at in the brief exposition here.

Having constructed the system and meanings of a German system of personal address, Winchatz (2001) shows how this system works in daily life, in terms of close relationships, public events, and workplace communication. With regard to the workplace, she provides accounts showing that how German workers address each other, with *du* or *Sie*, can have important consequences for personal satisfaction and workplace morale, especially in those settings in which the dominant system is not shared by all workers. Thus, from this small detail of daily life, we can see large-scale consequences in particular settings and arenas. In a later study, Winchatz (2007, p. 66) shows how a worker from the former East Germany came to the West shortly after German reunification and found, in her new workplace, what she experienced to be an aggressive use of the *du* form—she said it came too early in her work relationships for her comfort and, as a result, she experienced considerable distress that lasted for a very long time. See other work on local means and meanings in organizations in Baxter (1993) and in Hall and Valde (1995).

A second recent example of such research is the study by Sally O. Hastings (2001) of everyday and public communication among students from India who were studying at a large U.S. university. One of the concerns of such sojourners, as Hastings refers to them, is to adapt to their host society while yet retaining their sense of cultural integrity. They experience the normative and cultural pressures of the host society and, at the same time, the cross-pressures of other sojourners from the same country of origin. How can one come to understand the meanings and force of such cross-pressures in the lives of the individual sojourners? Hastings spent over a year observing and interviewing Indian students at the university in order to learn about the cross-pressures they experienced and of their ways of dealing with them.

The core of Hastings' research consists of intensive, exploratory interviews with sojourners, including repeat interviews of many of those who worked with her, as well as extensive observation of community events which sojourners planned and in which they participated. That is, her method involved a series of intense conversations with sojourners about their experience as well as direct observation of sojourner communicative conduct across a variety of settings that Hastings did not herself create or manage. Hastings' concern with the big picture involved filling in many small details, using the big picture as constructed to illumine such details but also using the details— particular communicative events, or sequences of acts and interpretations—to help understand and complete a more holistic portrayal of the sojourner experience.

One seemingly small matter was observed at a community event, for which Hastings had a videotape that permitted her to examine, and re-examine, some of the fine details of communicative conduct of the event. In a skit performed at India Night, an annual campus event organized by the Indian Student Association, one of the Indian graduate students performed a parody of another Indian student at the university who had expressed in public some of his concerns about his own adaptation to the local U.S. culture. At one point during the performance, the crowd responded to the speaker's parody with seven seconds of disapproving laughter, yells, and whistles that stopped the performance (seven seconds can seem like a long time in such a performance situation). Later Hastings transcribed this brief but poignant moment and then used her notes and recollections of over a year of fieldwork among these sojourners to explain why the performed identity that the speaker displayed evoked the strong and largely disapproving response that it did.

Working with her extensive collection of field materials, Hastings built an interpretation of the significance of the performance and of the audience's response to it. The substance of the performance was an Indian graduate student reflecting about how he might do things to draw attention to himself on campus as a means of establishing a persona for himself in a world in which he was a stranger. The performance evoked disapproving laughter as well as scorn because, as Hastings demonstrated, the performance highlighted the flaunting of two fundamental Indian principles of self-expression: (1) be who you are; and (2) be interdependent with others. The mock performance of an Indian speculating about how to gain attention by distinguishing himself in the host society violated both of these principles. Here the researcher focused on a means of communication, the public expression of speculation about self-adaptation to a host environment on the terms of the local culture, and the meaning of the actions that such expression would entail to the sojourners in terms of their homeland culture. Hastings' achievement in doing this exemplifies the work of the ethnographer of communication in exploring local practices of communicative conduct and their meanings to those who use and experience them. See other work on intercultural adaptation in Fong (1998) and Witteborn (2007).

As a third example, Evelyn Ho (Ho, 2006) spent eight months of full-time fieldwork studying communication at an acupuncture clinic in a city in the Pacific Northwest. The clinic, GFAC (an acronym for the pseudonymous Good Fortune Acupuncture Clinic), serves as a treatment center and as a training site for student interns from a local acupuncture college. There is one professional staff member at the clinic, a licensed acupuncturist, and Ho came into contact with 15 different interns there as part of her fieldwork. The clinic philosophy emphasizes a *Qi*-based approach that is considered to be a part of traditional Chinese medicine. Ho's specific point of inquiry was to discover whether the professional staff member and the 15 interns she encountered used a common way of speaking about their practice and, if so, what significance that way of speaking, as a means of communication, holds for participants in this community of practice.

Based on her extensive observational and interview materials, Ho found evidence of a systematic way of speaking about acupuncture that the professional acupuncturist and the interns used. Discovering and explicating this way of speaking provided a point of entry into the understanding of the nature and the meanings of the *Qi*-based practice that the students had learned and that was taught and practiced at the clinic, *Qi* being glossed as "life force" or "vital energy." Early in her fieldwork, Ho had seen an article in a popular American news magazine that cast acupuncture in a highly favorable light. She was initially surprised to learn that practitioners at the clinic were highly critical of the article. They acknowledged that the article treated their practice favorably, but complained that at the same time it badly misrepresented it. One specific complaint was that an essential component of traditional Chinese acupuncture, Qi, was mentioned, but without presenting the conceptual background that is necessary, they felt, to describe it accurately. A related complaint was that the article treated *Qi*-based acupuncture by comparing it to Western medicine. They felt that to do so is to fail to capture the essence of *Qi*-based acupuncture in its own terms.

Ho's study (2006) provides a descriptive and interpretive background that answers precisely the concerns that the *Qi*-based acupuncturists expressed about the way other outsiders characterized their practice, in that she, Ho, paid particular attention to the very terms and expressions that these practitioners use to talk about their practice. The opening insight that Ho produces, the complaint that others fail to describe the conceptual background to *Qi*, even though they "mention" it, to some ears a seemingly trivial expression, turns out to provide an approach to what the practitioners themselves consider to be a fundamental defining attribute of their practice, that is, that it is set against a conceptual background that provides the ideational context of *Qi*. From there, Ho turns to the expression "feel the *Qi*," an expression that is used to describe the practice itself, from the perspective of the practitioners, an expression that says something that glosses an experience at the heart of the practice. Furthermore, to speak of "feeling the *Qi*" and similar expressions with *Qi* in them is an indicator, to these practitioners, that someone has an insider's knowledge and experience of the approach they all practice. Finally, it is the elevation of a way of speaking that has expressions about *Qi* in them that differentiates among practitioners from different national traditions, specifically that differentiates Chinese, *Qi*-based acupuncturists, from acupuncturists trained in a Japanese tradition.

Thus far I have sketched a general portrait of an investigator searching to discover local means and meanings of communication, with the aid of extant descriptive resources that help the ethnographer to discover the particularities of communication in some particular locale. There is a further resource that the ethnographer uses for her or his investigative work and that is the now-large body of published work that is available on culturally distinctive ways of communicating, work that crosses many societies and many language varieties. Here I refer to a large collection of individual studies, based on particular times and places and on particular languages and other means of communication, all of which studies have been produced by ethnographers of communication across several disciplines, including anthropology, communication, education, folklore, history, and sociology. In 1962, Dell Hymes, a linguist, anthropologist, and folklorist, issued a call for such studies and provided a descriptive framework for conducting and reporting such studies. As previously mentioned, the 1962 framework has been modified, and extended, many times, but its core principles are still in active use. Twenty-four years after the 1962 call was made, Philipsen and Carbaugh (1986) made a record of some 250 subsequent published studies that could be traced to Hymes' earlier (1962) call. There is no systematic record of the number of such studies produced since 1986, but there can be little doubt that the number is at least equal to that earlier 24-year output, and there is a great deal of such work presently in progress.

The import of the record of published studies in the ethnography of communication is manifold. For one thing, the record constitutes an impressive body of knowledge of communication across dozens of languages and cultures. For another, the record speaks to the productivity of the enterprise of the ethnography of communication. And for the presently working ethnographers of communication, this body of published work is a resource that can be deployed to aid any given study to be undertaken. Here is how this works. At the most general level, each of the entries in the record contains in some form the story of a previous scholar's success in discovering the means and meanings of communication in some particular time and place. Thus, the record can be read as a source of insight into how to do the present work of discovering the particularities of a given time and place. If a present investigator plans to study how, in a given time and place, communication is talked about and thought about in terms of, for example, medical interactions, that investigator can consult the record to find out about whether and if so how such interactions have been studied ethnographically, in other times and places, with an exploratory eye and ear, and with a considered concern for means and meanings of communicative practice. Perhaps one finds, in such a search, that there is, or were, in some places—for example, Laotian villages—a rule against a physician smiling when he first encounters the patient (Fadiman, 1997). The present investigator can use such a cross-cultural insight by including in her scheme of awareness and observation the category of nonverbal communicative actions in greetings in initial medical encounters and then seek to discover whether there is a local means that people use and attend to and if so what its local meanings are.

The research strategy that I described in the previous paragraph consists of using past studies of similar phenomena to guide a present study, that is, of building upon past success to try to achieve present success. On one hand this involves using the descriptive frameworks that have been developed in the past, such as those developed by Hymes (1962, 1972), Philipsen (1987, 1992, 1997), Carbaugh, Gibson, and

Milburn (1997), and Philipsen, Coutu, and Covarrubias (2005), to help one conduct a present study. This is what Winchatz, Hastings, and Ho did. On the other hand, it involves using past studies of particular phenomena to guide present studies of particular phenomena. For example, in her studies of German personal address, Winchatz (2001) drew on past studies of personal address in the U.S. (Sequeira, 1993), Colombia (Fitch, 1998), and Mexico (Covarrubias, 2002). Hastings (2001) drew on past studies of social dramas and community discussion of proper communicative conduct such as those of Carbaugh (1990) and Philipsen (1986). Ho (2006) drew on past studies of traditional medicine (Tonelli & Callahan, 2001) and of the role of common ways of speaking as constituting a speech community (Fitch, 1994) to develop her interpretation of the nature and social functions of a *Qi*-based speech code.

The above is a brief description of the approach to the study of communication that is taken by a network of scholars in the discipline of communication. Next, I turn to that network, to describe it and to suggest some of the work it has done and is capable of doing.

A NETWORK OF SCHOLARS IN THE DISCIPLINE OF COMMUNICATION

The nature of the volume in which this chapter appears provides the rationale for reporting and commenting here on the emergence, over the past 30 years, of a network of scholars, trained in and working in the discipline of communication. The volume is addressed, most particularly, to two audiences. One of these is people and organizations that seek to advance knowledge through targeted research projects that show promise for addressing important needs and concerns in contemporary society. The other audience is prospective students who seek to become research scholars in communication and who therefore wish to ascertain what some of the styles and approaches of research are being pursued and for which one can be educated as a scholar.

To both of the audiences mentioned above, I would say: There is a network of scholars within the discipline who are capable and experienced to conduct the sort of research that is desired; the participants in this network are actively contributing important scholarship using the approach described here; and there is within this network a cluster of graduate programs that have strong records in producing scholars who are competent to use this approach, as attested, for example by having their work published in highly competitive, peer-reviewed journals such as *Research on Language and Social Interaction*, the journal that published the studies by Winchatz, Hastings, and Ho as referenced above.

First, I will mention the opportunities for graduate study. This is potentially important for someone seeking to enroll in a graduate program but also important for those who seek to recruit scholars from such programs. There are many good programs within the communication discipline for the ethnographic study of communication in the descriptive–comparative tradition. Although I will mention some of these, I do not mean to imply that there are not others that are worthy of mention, rather I emphasize those with which I am most familiar.

There are four doctoral programs within the discipline that have, for the past ten to thirty years, educated strong doctoral researchers in the descriptive–comparative ethnographic approach to the study of communication. These are, in alphabetical order, the University of Haifa (Israel), and, in the U.S., the Universities of Iowa, Massachusetts-Amherst, and Washington. Each of these programs is located within a department of communication; provides doctoral level study in the approach; and has produced multiple doctoral-level researchers who have published scholarly books and published widely in peer-reviewed scholarly journals.[1]

If we take just these four programs together, considering the ethnographic research of the faculty and the doctoral students in them, there is published work that has been conducted in 17 different language varieties and 16 different countries. For the study in any one country or in any one language variety, the typical time of fieldwork is approximately one year of full-time in-country research for data collection. This research is concentrated in the U.S. (a site of multiple cultures and language varieties), Israel, and several Latin American countries and varieties of Spanish. But there is also work in several European and Asian countries and languages. Later in the chapter I describe a new initiative that gives promising initial evidence that it is possible to secure important ethnographic learning in less than our customary one year of fieldwork.

There are two ways that the research of this group has contributed—and can continue to contribute—new knowledge about communication. One is through the study of ways of communicating in particular sites. Thus, we have produced a great deal of knowledge about cultural aspects of communication in the U.S., Israel, Finland, Colombia, Mexico, Germany, to mention a few places. Reviews of our findings by people who live in these countries and speak the local languages suggest that our scholars succeeded in providing explanations of cultural conduct that had previously been puzzling to insiders and that pass other tests of insider validation. A second and related way is that we have used the results of the particular studies as sources of data for generating theory, for answering general questions about communication. Our collective corpus of ethnographic data is, so far as I know, the largest extant collection of cross-linguistic, cross-cultural data available on which to ground a theoretical understanding of communication. These synthetic and theoretical findings have been published in the forms of cross-cultural comparative analyses (e.g., Braithwaite, 1990; Carbaugh, 1989; Carbaugh, Boromisza-Habashi, & Ge, 2006; Goldsmith, 1990; Philipsen, 1989b) and in theoretical statements about how, in general, communication works (Hall, 1992; Philipsen, 1997; Philipsen, Coutu, & Covarrubias, 2005). One of the cross-linguistic, cross-cultural theoretical insights we have been able to produce is basic knowledge about how to go about learning another culture's code for communicative conduct. Based on our collective experience, we can teach someone how to do this. This is stated in theoretical form in Philipsen (1997) as proposition four and in Philipsen, Coutu, and Covarrubias (2005) as proposition five. Should anyone publish evidence that challenges this proposition and, by implication, the basis of some of our best practical advice, we would be very interested to learn from such new data. All of our empirical and theoretical claims are always open to revision in the light of critique, and we are especially interested in experiential and empirical-based critiques. We are not married to our theoretical conclusions.

FROM RESEARCH TO THEORY TO PRACTICE

The work of this network of researchers began as research into particular sites and the means and meanings of communication that could be found there (for book-length examples, see Carbaugh, 1988, 2005; Covarrubias, 2002; Fitch, 1998; Katriel, 1986; Philipsen, 1992). To enter a site, study it, and then learn something reportable about communication there is always quite a ride. But from the beginning of the group's work we have also been interested in developing theories grounded in our fieldwork data (Carbaugh, Gibson, & Milburn, 1997; Hall, 1992; Philipsen, 1992, 1997; Philipsen, Coutu, & Covarrubias 2005). More recently, participants in the network have increasingly been asked to participate in research projects, or have generated their own, in which there is the hope that ethnographic research into communication could directly address important human needs. We are now sufficiently advanced that we can make important contributions in this way. For the past ten years, participants in the group have worked as researchers in projects in schools of medicine, engineering, nursing, education, and in other applied and professional domains. These are all projects in which the founders and funders have hoped that social research such as ours could contribute to the illumination and amelioration of social concerns. Here I mention two in-process projects that illustrate this recent, more applied move by participants in our network, collaborating with others.

First, for many, perhaps most people in the world today there is a need and a desire to learn about their own and others' ways of communicating in culturally distinctive ways. For example, there are many countries, organizations, and individuals who wish to enter into the lives of other countries, organizations, and individuals so as to work with them constructively in joint projects. This requires the visitors, as it were, to learn something about the local culture, and in many instances they do not know how to do this as effectively as they would like to do. More broadly, this is the problem of effective communication across cultures.

Two researchers who are part of our network have initiated an innovative program to assist, through research, in the process of effective communication across cultures, in difficult situations. Derek Miller, a Ph.D. in political science, and Lisa Rudnick, a doctoral candidate in communication at the University of Massachusetts, have for six years worked to develop and implement this program, through which they have built and demonstrated a new way to do in-country research into local cultures that can help to improve the operational effectiveness of international agencies in humanitarian, development, and security operations in local communities (Miller & Rudnick, 2008). Their immediate project is the Security Needs Assessment Protocol (or, the acronym SNAP), a systematic approach to research into local cultures that they have field-tested now in two countries, Ghana and Nepal. At the theoretical heart of the project is the theoretical apparatus that has been developed by our network of scholars in the communication discipline and, thus, it emphasizes paying explicit attention to local means and meanings of communication, with special attention, in this phase, to local vocabularies pertaining to "security" needs and the structure of understandings that are expressible through those vocabularies.

Preliminary work by the SNAP team provides evidence that the application of its protocol has significant promise for producing rapid, valid, and practically valuable learnings about local understandings of security. The initial reception of their early findings, both locally in the sites of inquiry and internationally by funding agencies of several nations, suggests that they have made a significant advance in the

development of a methodology for contributing to cross-cultural understandings in situations where such understandings are vital to the
well-being of local communities that experience difficult conflicts and
that seek to minimize the harmful effects of those conflicts on local
populations. The SNAP team's work also has considerable promise for
the development of the broader methodology and theoretical perspective of the communication-discipline based network of ethnography of
communication researchers.

A second example is found in the work of Deborah Bassett, a doctoral student in the ethnography of communication at the University
of Washington. She is working on a National Science Foundation-
sponsored project on social and ethical issues in developments in the
new interdisciplinary field of nanoscience. In the face of claims, by
prominent nanoscientists, that nanoscience has the potential to change
dramatically many aspects of human life, there has been expressed
strong concerns about whether the social and ethical aspects of such
new developments in knowledge are being considered adequately. This
has given rise to multiple research projects in the U.S. that are concerned with how these aspects are, or are not, being discussed and
considered. Bassett's particular project, including her doctoral dissertation in communication (in progress), is concerned at the descriptive
level with listening to how nanoscientists themselves talk about their
work and to ask: (1) whether there can be heard in such talk a "code,"
as it were, about such work; and, if so, (2) of what does that code
consist? Put in the terms of this chapter, this is a matter of investigating whether there is a means of communication—that is, a way of
speaking—that can be found in the talk of nanoscientists about their
work. To report briefly, and in only a very preliminary way about
Bassett's findings, I can say that one important part of the news is that,
indeed, among these scientists there can be found such a code. Furthermore, the code as expressed reveals a strong disposition to warn
against, even to preclude, serious talk about the social and ethical issues
of the potential social implications of the development of such a science. Bassett works to discover, to delineate, to analyze, and to interpret
this way of speaking (or way of speaking about not speaking), and to
find in it a code that can be understood and engaged as an important
part of a larger project to hold a productive social conversation about
these potentially important social implications.

The two examples given above can only hint at the richness of the
two projects that are mentioned and these two projects themselves are
but a few of the many such applied moves being made by ethnographers of communication in the communication discipline. It seems that

everywhere one might turn to consider social processes and social concerns, there is a need for local understandings in general and a need for understanding the local means of communication and the meanings of those means to those who use and experience them. We are discovering this need, in studies of intimate and family life, organizational work, community dialogues and forums, the understanding of communication technologies, and communication about science and technology, as well as the problems and prospects of communication across and within local cultures. To these many situations and concerns, we offer a modest contribution, an approach to the study of communication from a local ethnographic perspective, a network of scholars who can help to make that contribution, and a series of places where this approach is being taught and, of course, held up to critical examination.

NOTE

1. There are scholars who earned their doctorates in one of these four programs who are now on the communication faculties of other institutions where the doctorate in communication is offered. These include the University of Colorado-Boulder, the University of New Mexico, and the Chinese University of Hong Kong. Mention should also be made of strong programs in the ethnography of communication in departments of communication at the University of Illinois at Champaign-Urbana and at the University of Oklahoma.

REFERENCES

Albert, E. M. (1964). "Rhetoric," "logic," and "poetics" in Burundi: culture patterning of speech behavior. In J. J. Gumperz, & D. Hymes (Eds.), The ethnography of communication. *American Anthropologist, 66*, pt. 2(6), 35–54.

Baxter, L. A. (1993). "Talking things through" and "putting it in writing": Two codes of communication in an academic institution. *Journal of Applied Communication Research, 21*, 313–326.

Braithwaite, C. (1990). Communicative silence: A crosscultural study of Basso's hypothesis. In D. Carbaugh (Ed.), *Cultural communication and intercultural contact* (pp. 321–327). Hillsdale, NJ: Lawrence Erlbaum.

Carbaugh, D. (1987). Communication rules in Donahue discourse. *Research on Language and Social Interaction, 21*, 31–62.

Carbaugh, D. (1988). *Talking American.* New Jersey: Ablex.

Carbaugh, D. (1989). Fifty terms for talk: A cross-cultural study. *International and Intercultural Communication Annual, 13*, 93–120.

Carbaugh, D. (1990) *Cultural communication and intercultural contact.* Hillsdale, NJ: Lawrence Erlbaum Publishers.

Carbaugh, D. (1993). "Soul" and "self": Soviet and American cultures in conversation. *Quarterly Journal of Speech, 79*, 182–200.

Carbaugh, D. (1996). *Situating selves: The communication of social identities in American scenes.* Albany, NY: State University of New York Press.

Carbaugh, D. (2005). *Cultures in conversation.* Mahwah, NJ: Lawrence Erlbaum.

Carbaugh, D., Boromisza-Habashi, D., & Ge, X. (2006). Dialogue in cross-cultural perspective: Deciphering communication codes. In N. Aalto, & W. Reuter (Eds.), *Aspects of intercultural dialogue: Theory research applications* (pp.27–46). Köln: SAXA Verlag.

Carbaugh, D., Gibson, T., & Milburn, T. (1997). A view of communication and culture: Scenes in an ethnic cultural center and a private college. In B. Kovacic (Ed.), *Emerging theories of human communication* (pp. 1–24). Albany, NY: State University of New York Press.

Covarrubias, P. (2002). *Culture, communication, and cooperation: Interpersonal relations and pronominal address in a Mexican organization.* Lanham, MD: Rowman & Littlefield.

Fadiman, A. (1997). *The spirit catches you and you fall down: A Hmong child, her American doctors, and the collision of two cultures.* New York: Farrar, Straus & Giroux.

Fitch, K. (1994). The issue of selection of objects of analysis in ethnographies of speaking. *Research on Language and Social Interaction, 27*, 51–93.

Fitch, K. (1998). *Speaking relationally: Culture, communication, and interpersonal communication.* New York: Guilford Press.

Fong, M. (1998). Chinese immigrants' perceptions of semantic dimensions of direct/indirect communication in intercultural compliment interactions with North Americans. *Howard Journal of Communication, 9*, 245–262.

Goldsmith, D. (1989/1990). Gossip from the native's point of view: A comparative analysis. *Research on Language and Social Interaction, 23*, 163–194.

Hall, B. (1988/1989). Norms, action, and alignment: A discursive perspective. *Research on Language and Social Interaction, 22*, 23–44.

Hall, B. (1992). Theories of culture and communication. *Communication Theory, 2*, 50–70.

Hall, B., & Valde, K. (1995). Brown-nosing as a cultural category in American organizational life. *Research on Language and Social Interaction, 22*, 391–419.

Hastings, S. O. (2001). Social drama as a site for the communal construction and management of Asian Indian "stranger" identity. *Research on Language and Social Interaction, 34*, 309–336.

Ho, E. (2006). Behold the power of Qi: The importance of Qi in the discourse of acupuncture. *Research on Language and Social Interaction, 39*, 411–440.

Hymes, D. (1962). The ethnography of speaking. In T. Gladwin, & W. C. Sturtevant (Eds.), *Anthropology and human behavior* (pp. 13–53).

Washington, DC: Anthropological Society of Washington. (Reprinted in *Readings in the sociology of language*, pp. 99–137, J. Fishman, Ed., 1968, Paris: Mouton).

Hymes, D. (1972). Models of the interaction of language and social life. In J. J. Gumperz, & D. Hymes (Eds.), *Directions in sociolinguistics: The ethnography of communication* (pp. 35–71). New York: Holt, Rinehart and Winston.

Katriel, T. (1986). *Talking straight: "Dugri" speech in Israeli Sabra culture.* Cambridge: Cambridge University Press.

Leeds-Hurwitz, W. (1990). Culture as communication: A review essay, *Quarterly Journal of Speech, 76*, 85–116.

Miller, D., & Rudnick, L. (2008). *The security needs assessment protocol: Improving operational effectiveness through community security.* New York and Geneva: United Nations Publications.

Murray, S. (1993). *Theory groups and the study of language in North America: A social history.* Amsterdam: John Benjamins Publishing Company.

Philipsen, G. (1987). The prospect for cultural communication. In D. Kincaid (Ed.), *Communication theory from Eastern and Western perspectives* (pp. 245–254). San Diego, CA: Academic Press.

Philipsen, G. (1989a). An ethnographic approach to communication studies. In B. Dervin (Ed.), *Paradigm dialogues: Research exemplars* (pp. 258–268). Newbury Park, CA: Sage.

Philipsen, G. (1989b). Speaking as a communal resource in four cultures. *International and Intercultural Communication Annual, 13*, 79–92.

Philipsen, G. (1992). *Speaking culturally: Explorations in social communication.* Albany, NY: State University of New York Press.

Philipsen, G. (1997). A theory of speech codes. In G. Philipsen, & T. L. Albrecht (Eds.), *Developing communication theories* (pp. 119–156). Albany, NY: SUNY.

Philipsen, G., & Carbaugh, D. (1986). A bibliography of fieldwork in the ethnography of communication. *Language in Society, 15*, 387–398.

Philipsen, G., Coutu, L., & Covarrubias, P. (2005). Speech codes theory: Restatement, revisions, and response to criticisms. In W. Gudykunst (Ed.), *Theorizing about intercultural communication* (pp. 55–68). Thousand Oaks, CA: Sage.

Sequeira, D. (1993). Personal address as negotiated meaning in an American church community. *Research on Language and Social Interaction, 26*, 259–285.

Smith III, R. E. (1992). Hymes, Rorty, and the social-rhetorical construction of meaning, *College English, 54*, 138–158.

Tonelli, M. R., & Callahan, T. C. (2001). Why alternative medicine cannot be evidence-based. *Academic Medicine, 767*, 1213–1220.

Winchatz, M. (2001). Social meanings in German interactions: An ethnographic analysis of the second-person pronoun *Sie. Research on Language and Social Interaction, 34*, 337–369.

Winchatz, M. (2007). German pronominal systems in conflict: The discursive negotiation of *du* and *Sie*. *International Journal of Communication, 17,* 55–78.

Witteborn, S. (2007). The expression of Palestinian identity in narratives about personal experiences: Implications for the study of narrative, identity, and social interaction. *Research on Language and Social Interaction, 40,* 145–170.

SUGGESTED READINGS

Philosophy and Theory

Flyvbjerg, B. (2001). *Making social science matter: why social inquiry fails and how it can succeed again.* Cambridge: Cambridge University Press.

Hymes, D. (1962). The ethnography of speaking. In T. Gladwin, & W. Sturtevant (Eds.), *Anthropology and human behavior* (pp. 13–53). Washington, DC: Anthropological Society of Washington.

Hymes, D. (1972). Models of the interaction of language and social life. In J. Gumperz, & D. Hymes (Eds.), *Directions in sociolinguistics: The ethnography of communication* (pp. 35–71). New York: Holt, Rinehart, and Winston.

Philipsen, G. (1987). The prospect for cultural communication. In L. Kincaid (Ed.), *Communication theory: Eastern and Western perspectives* (pp. 245–254). New York: Academic Press.

Philipsen, G. (1997). A theory of speech codes. In G. Philipsen, & T. Albrecht (Eds.), *Developing communication theories* (pp. 119–156). Albany, NY: State University of New York Press.

Philipsen, G. (2002). Cultural communication. In W. Gudykunst, & B. Mody (Eds.), *Handbook of international and intercultural communication* (pp. 51–67). Thousand Oaks, CA: Sage.

Methodology

Gumperz, J. (1992). Interviewing in intercultural situations. In P. Drew, & J. Heritage (Eds.), *Talk at work: Interaction in institutional settings* (pp. 302–327). Cambridge: Cambridge University Press.

Hymes, D. (1996). *Ethnography, linguistics, narrative inequality: Toward an understanding of voice.* New York: Taylor and Francis.

Philipsen, G. (1977). Linearity of research design in ethnographic studies of speaking. *Communication Quarterly, 25,* 42–50.

Applications

Carbaugh, D. (2005). *Cultures in conversation.* Mahwah, NJ: Lawrence Erlbaum Associates.

Covarrubias, P. (2002). *Culture, communication, and cooperation: Interpersonal relations and pronominal address in a Mexican organization.* Lanham, MD: Rowan and Littlefield.

Fitch, K. (1998). *Speaking relationally: Culture and interpersonal communication in Colombia.* New York: Guilford Press.

Katriel, T. (2004). *Dialogic moments: From soul talks to talk radio in Israeli culture.* Detroit, MI: Wayne State University Press.

7

REFLECTIONS ON DISTINCTIVE QUALITIES IN COMMUNICATION RESEARCH

Donal Carbaugh and Patrice M. Buzzanell

When studying communication, scholars focus on some types of data and do so from some particular point of view. At this moment of our intellectual history, communication data can be generated virtually everywhere including face-to-face encounters, online news and comedy, through a variety of mobile technologies, in linguistic and non-linguistic ways, including visual and acoustical signals. What the most salient data are, how they are identified, and what can be said about them are questions communication scholars, in the course of their studies, raise and address. These are important concerns because, as scholars consider them, their studies gain their toe-hold so-to-speak, through "data," in personal and social realities. While collecting and analyzing data are crucial parts of the research process, there is much more involved than this, or much more surrounding these specific decisions.

From what perspective are data being generated, organized, interpreted, and/or explained? It is possible, of course, to collect, and then account for communication data (such as public reports about smoking, or cancer, or step-families) from a variety of perspectives. For example, data can be utilized as a manifestation of political and economic factors, as an expression of psychological states or traits, or as an outcome of social class or cultural structures. If considered in these ways, these communication phenomena would be explained from the view of political, economic, psychological, sociological, or anthropological theories, respectively. Each of these disciplinary perspectives would provide important insights and accounts, but each would not be exactly the same as communicational explanations. How does one produce communicational explanations of phenomena? Communication scholars believe that communication has a hand in shaping aspects of human existence and that this process can be studied in its own right and not simply as a means of investigating other phenomena.

For the scholars whose works are assembled here, we note that communication is not only the data of concern, but is also, and moreover, the primary theoretical concern. We note this dual emphasis, on communication data *and* theory, as twin bases on which to begin our reflections about what indeed are some distinctive qualities in their Communication Research. We want to emphasize, initially, that the research reported above, and examined here explores the world not just as communication data. Rather, the research further understands data from the perspective of communication theory. A similar point was introduced long ago, early last century by the Pragmatist William James who noted that communication is a double-barreled term: it is both a practice, but it is moreover a perspective on that practice. We have been working since to understand all the implications of James's double-barreled thought!

Our reflections in this chapter are designed to summarize, generally, five qualities that are distinctive in the communication research discussed in this volume. We organize these as five reflections that elaborate specific concerns of research design: (1) conceptualizing the researcher's concerns as communication concerns; (2) addressing social problems as communication problems; (3) asking research questions about communication; (4) using a methodology that is based upon communication theory and data; and (5) accounting for findings from the perspective of communication practices and theory, that is, demonstrating how communication is formative in structuring, or giving order to, social and cultural lives. In what follows we summarize each of these qualities as reflections upon the communication research assembled here.

In our reflections, we treat each author's work in a summary form, rather than delving into the details of their theories and research as it has been written into their contributions. We note that the authors' works do not, in the whole nor does each of their studies in part, necessarily include all five qualities, but some of their works, here and elsewhere, do. As a result, we introduce an important caveat. We are discussing a range of possibilities in various types of communication research. Our comments are *not* intended as a requirement that all research has all of the five qualities discussed here. Our purpose is primarily reflective, not legislative! At the same time we would add that all five qualities, if present, can create a robustly designed communication study.

QUALITY 1, THEORETICAL PERSPECTIVE: CONCEPTUALIZING CONCERNS AS COMMUNICATION

We find it instructive to review how the authors in this book conceptualize their concerns as communication concerns. In other words, we ask: when the authors look upon the world as communication scholars, how do they see, hear, and/or feel it?

Leslie Baxter sees the concerns she researches as the "interactive process of meaning making," and as an "interdependence of messages." This process and this interdependence involve at times the "struggle among and between different discourses." From her approach, she gives special attention to where discourses come from (i.e., their history), how they are being used in present communication events, and what might be said next. Her concerns bring into play multiple discourses, "inter-textual" relationships, and how utterances can play dialectically one with others. As she studies communication, she draws our attention to various personal, social, and cultural concerns, understands these as the interaction of messages which are potentially dense with meanings, potential sites of struggle and difference, all of this being constitutive of our social lives yet open to further negotiation.

Stan Deetz states a similar view of "communication as constitutive of identities, difference, [and] power relations." He argues that some of the social problems of our day—including the problems of difference and social interdependence—can benefit from such a conceptualization. His treatment of the constitutive role of communication argues that the social process of communication precedes the personal sense of the world. This view renders knowledge, facts, and perception not as prior to communication, but as social outcomes of communication systems, even though these may be experienced as "presocial realities." Deetz argues similarly that subjective states are also outcomes of communication processes as one sees and experiences in ways that are tutored, *a priori*, by a communication order. One of the tasks of this conceptualization, then, according to Deetz and kindred others, is uncovering just how communication has indeed led to this ordering of knowledge and experience in social and subjective lives. Through discussions of Habermas, Deetz elaborates his critical view that political, or class-based dynamics are co-existent with these processes since power is "ever-present" in them. Positive developments are needed, Deetz argues, which embrace positive social relations through unveiling various communicative sites of discursive contestation, freeing them for scrutiny and change.

Michael Hecht discusses his view of "communication as culturally situated message design and interpretation." He focuses upon culturally-based message design and its effects. Hecht is particularly concerned not just with the nature of message design, but moreover with the specific forms possible for the design of the message. Possibilities are indeed multiple in any one occasion for the "forming" of messages and it is the study of this variety, and the tailoring of it for a particular social and cultural context that are of concern in his large-scale studies. The narrative form of communication, as well as personal stories, plays a special role in his approach. While all people tell stories, Hecht recognizes that their ingredients, the characters, the plot lines, the dramatic actions, their resolution, and so on are situationally managed and culturally distinct. His approach then draws attention to local practices, identities, taken-for-granted knowledge, dynamics of belonging, inter-group dynamics, various cross-cultural dimensions of each, with each, when explored in context, helping to target messages about health to specific peoples and contexts.

Joseph Cappella and Robert Hornik take communication to be "a practical science of messages and their specific consequences." Their goal is to isolate specific abstract features of messages and their consequences. The approach they adopt is deeply theory-driven, directed to isolating abstract dimensions of messages and asking why they have the specific consequences that they do. Conducting research in this way enables the investigators to provide practical, and a-cultural knowledge about communication, how it works generally, as well as how it can best be designed for specific purposes and effects. In their studies, they address several important social problems which we will examine in more detail below. They seek to create practical communicative action which can meet three general criteria: It is a practice that reaches targeted populations, effectively achieves its desired objectives (in form and content), and does so efficiently (providing maximum benefit at the lowest cost). Cappella and Hornik's approach offers a highly productive conceptualization of communication as a practical and general "science of messages and their specific consequences."

Gerry Philipsen conceptualizes "communication as culturally distinctive means and meanings." His focus is on the ethnographic discovery of local means of communication including any available means being used by community members; the concern is also with explicating the meanings these means of communication have to participants themselves. Traditionally ethnographers of communication, as Philipsen discusses, have understood the social world as a set of communication events, communication situations, or ways of speaking. Out of these conceptualizations have been developed additional concepts that explore and explain communication as a variety of speech codes and cultural discourses. Philipsen reviews a network of scholars' works that demonstrate a variety of ethnographic concerns such as the cultural uses and meanings of pronouns, the cultural drama of sojourner and diasporic identity, and the cultural conception and treatment of health. Each demonstrates the philosophical commitment to discovering "local means and meanings of communication," yet does so through a general, developing theoretical perspective that is being used and developed by this network of scholars. A goal of the network is accumulating a body of work that is available for consultation, and heuristically employed in their subsequent cooperative, collaborative, and cross-cultural research.

What makes communication research distinctive? One response is this: It is the conceptualization brought to its study. The conceptualizations of the above authors treat personal, social, and cultural lives, respectively, as communication processes of meaning-making, as formative of identities (differences and power relations), as culturally situated message design and interpretation, as a practical science of messages and their specific consequences, or as culturally distinctive means and meanings of expression. The world can and has been studied as such, as grandly complex communication phenomena, with some real—practical and theoretical—benefit, which we turn to next.

QUALITIES 2–3, PROBLEMS AND PROBES: SOCIAL ISSUES AND ASKING ABOUT COMMUNICATION

What kinds of social problems are the authors addressing? What and how do they pose research questions about those problems?

Reflecting upon the scholars' works included here takes us into explorations of many of the important social problems and issues of our age. Yet for each, it is not just the specific significance of the problem being raised that is important, nor its prominence as a social problem, but how it is probed that distinguishes the works gathered here as communication research. The research questions posed and pursued are crucially important to reflect upon. So we ask: what problems are being addressed, and how are questions being posed about that problem?

Consider Leslie Baxter's works. In her studies, among other concerns, she asks us to think carefully about step-families, teen pregnancy, and alcohol use. She suggests a range of important questions about these by asking how people talk about alcohol use and teen pregnancy, and how discourse is structuring life in step-families. Note that these questions are posed not only to explore the topic of teen pregnancy and the like, but to create knowledge about the role of communication in structuring that topic, identities, and social relations. By so asking, she positions her studies to reveal discourses that create dialectical dynamics concerning, for example, pregnancy and alcohol use. In this way of probing, communication does not simply *reflect* relational dynamics, but is *openly constitutive* of people's relations as they deal with issues such as pregnancy and alcohol use.

Stan Deetz raises concerns about diversity and differences in the life of a society; he advocates inquiry about the role of power relations in understanding and addressing those concerns. Questions are suggested about how communication is practiced in a way such that some groups are being disadvantaged, or ethnic differences are being communicatively cast as negative rather than positive, or capitalist organizations are interactionally naturalized rather than problematized, or psychological states are treated expressively as given rather than being socially constituted. Deetz demonstrates how social problems of power and preference can and should be probed through questions like these, about communication as formative of differences, relations of dominance, and the like.

Michael Hecht addresses crucially important large-scale social problems surrounding health care and education. He asks how communication plays a role in portraying health in a particular way, for example, how smoking is expressed among teens in a city. He asks further, after knowing this, how communication can be designed to decrease the rate of teen smoking in such a community. The questions posed address crucial social problems, yet they do so in a theoretically focused, systematic, and large-scale way. Hecht's investigations, in other words, not only probe important social health problems, but do so by asking how communication is being structured to conceive of, interpret, and address those problems.

Joseph Cappella and Robert Hornik ask also about specific health concerns such as smoking, obesity, and the ways genetic health risks are discussed. Their approach is focused on specific yet abstract rather than cultural features of messages. These aspects of messages, they argue, have specific and traceable consequences. Their approach asks questions of "why and how" these features of messages work exactly as they do. The objective is creating propositions which "represent causal claims that have a truth value well beyond their context and historical period of application." For example, it is crucial to know, according to Cappella and Hornik, exactly whether specific outcomes co-vary with a "loss frame" and a "gain frame" in health messages, and whether these frames are being mediated by emotional processes such as anxiety, fear, and/or apprehension. Asking about specific features of messages, how they co-vary with others, and why they work as they do provides propositional knowledge about messages, and their consequences. These probes are crucial to pose not only for advancing our understanding of health issues such as smoking and genetic health risks, but also for developing a scientific and practical knowledge of how communication can be designed more effectively and efficiently for specific target populations.

Gerry Philipsen asks about the local means, and the meanings of communicating in specific human communities. He reviews a range of studies that address important social problems from levels of solidarity and intimacy within communities, to managing identity across cultural scenes, to basic interpretations of health and its treatment. Philipsen discusses two ongoing large-scale ethnographic research projects that are addressing issues of community security in Ghana, Nepal, and elsewhere, and the conduct of science among nano-scientists—and whether scientists say ethics should be included in their talk about their science. The ethnographic studies raise crucial social issues of difference, identity, health, security, science, and ethics while also generating an understanding of the ways communication locally structures the means and meanings of communicating about them in specific scenes.

What is distinctive, then, as communication research across these cases? Coupled with an impressive attentiveness to prominent social problems today, are the ways each can be probed. These scholars see communication as having a hand in forming conceptions of the social problem itself, as the process which gives it particularity in shape and meaning. They open the door to understanding how communication itself structures the public meanings of the social matter, and thus ask about each as not only an end product but as a result of a process of communication. Doing so deeply grounds investigations of these social problems in communication. As a result, and adding this point to the first quality above, social problems of our day are coupled not only with scholarly probes about, but theoretical perspectives of communication. Together, this helps contribute a communicational view to researching the matters at hand.

QUALITY 4, PROCEDURES: METHODOLOGY AND INQUIRING ABOUT COMMUNICATION

Our authors vary about whether methodology generally carries any particular accent when done in the context of communication research. Leslie Baxter, Michael Hecht, and others suggest that other researchers in other fields also do scientific study, qualitative research, field research, and/or ethnography as do communication scholars. In some sense, then, a particular method, like interviewing, may not be distinctive at a general level. But then, how the interviewing is designed, about what, may indeed be distinctive as part of a larger methodology. Along this line of thought, Michael Hecht suggests that perhaps a synthetic attentiveness to concerns which others tend to keep separate, such as designing methods attentive to communication and culture, may give communication scholars a distinctive accent in their design of research methodologies.

We want to suggest that research methodology is for some deeply tied to theoretical concerns. In this sense, if one has conceptualized concerns of study as communication concerns, for example, as the process of message design and interpretation, and if one is asking in one's research about communication practices, processes, or principles, then in some sense, at another level, the methodology one employs is itself distinctive as communication scholarship. If one is theorizing a dynamic of health delivery as "interactional message design," then one's methodology includes data that are, in some sense, or should be, "interactional." Or, if one is asking about discourses of power, then one's basic data should include a systematic examination of discursive data that exhibits, and systematically examines, power.

To reiterate, if a scholar is conceptualizing a phenomenon and developing research questions about it as communication, then one's data, the variety of data needed, and procedures for analyzing it will be somewhat distinctive as communication. Qualitative research, in particular, can examine what indeed are local, or salient events and processes of communication, as well as how these are related to a problem of investigation; probes can address how each communication event is the same as well as different from other events and processes. Quantitative research, in particular, can ask about the frequency and distribution, for example, of events and processes; how does each vary across sample and target populations? Each methodology, when turned to questions of communication has a distinctive role as it asks about communication phenomena and explores their nature, functions, and meanings, in theory and methodology.

Michael Hecht pushes a bit further, as do several others' discussions of collaborative group- and team-research. From the view of communication, an additional, reflexive dimension is possible. In other words, a communication researcher may not only explore the topic at hand such as security and teen pregnancy, but moreover can reflect upon the social process of conducting the research itself—as a communication process. Reflecting in this way can add further understanding to the social aspects of the research process itself. Researchers may ask: How are "we" researching this together, and how is this process an affordance and/or a hindrance to our study? This reflexive methodology is part of what may be offered by communication specialists to the process of doing research in teams, for the research is not only about communication but through a social process of communication itself. Research processes, then, can be understood in this way, as an additional subject for reflexive inquiry, the results of the reflection being used in the construction of further methodology, and thus benefiting from these insights about the conduct of the research team itself.

What makes a methodology distinctive as communication research? It is conceptualized to study communication, generates data that are communication, and formulates procedures for analyzing data as communication—possibly reflecting upon the research itself—as part of a complex communication process.

QUALITY 5, EXPLANATIONS: POSITING COMMUNICATION AS FORMATIVE OF SOCIAL AND CULTURAL LIFE

One reading of the above might suggest, as Kenneth Burke, William James, Susanne Langer, and Edward Sapir did long ago, that communication is understood as a primary social process, as the raw stuff of making more than the mere revealing of society. But can studying it help us interpret or explain anything? The authors here respond with a resounding "yes!"

Leslie Baxter uses the concept of discourse to account for various personal and social arrangements among families, teens, and tense moments. The latter are accounted for by formulating different and possibly contesting discourses, each positioning utterances and users in particular ways. Explaining the dynamics in this way, places them in a realm to be scrutinized, thus available for reflection and possible revision. The concept, discourse, and dialectics, help not only account for structure but also variation in personal and social lives. It offers further, from Baxter's view, an open space for reflection and possible changes.

Stan Deetz argues that communication generally, organizational and mass communication specifically, can be understood as deeply constitutive of social and personal lives. Conceived at the nexus of power and social construction, communication itself can explain received views of knowledge, of truth, of political structure. Through communication, such phenomena from knowledge to politics have been created, and unveiling the intricacies of this process offers a communicative explanation of knowledge, politics, and various other concerns.

Michael Hecht is able to explain the efficacy, or lack thereof, of large-scale health campaigns by positing culturally based views of message design, interpretation, and their effects. If an anti-smoking campaign succeeds, or fails, Hecht is able to identify cultural elements in, for example, the message form, or extant narratives, as reasons for this effect. In the process, communication has some explanatory power in the understanding and creation of health care and education. Cappella and Hornik examine health as well, but do so by formulating more general principles, focused on specific abstract features of messages, and the ways these co-vary, as principled explanations of messages' effectiveness in target populations.

Gerry Philipsen's ethnographic studies suggest interpretive accounts, and explanations through other concepts. A community's means and meanings of communication may reveal a code, or codes, through which a specific configuration of beliefs and values are active. The code may be active in communication events, or processes, and when so creates and presupposes certain meanings about social and cultural life. Of course, codes can be contested, and negotiated, situated or unsettled, as the drama of sojourner identity exhibits, but in any case when there is communication, according to this view, there are traces of culture that are active in that communication. Formulating a communication code, codes, or cultural discourses, is a way of describing, interpreting, and/or explaining through what means, and with what meanings communication is locally active.

So, what is distinctive as a communicative explanation? Each author, as others, has developed a technical vocabulary that is used for descriptive and explanatory purposes. As the latter, accounts are developed for interpreting, and explaining phenomena as the consequence of a communication process. In this way, various accounts are offered about important social phenomena such as stepfamilies, teens and alcohol, differences and power relations, health campaigns, obesity and smoking, security and science. Something significant and important can be said about each not merely as a topic for discussion, but as the result of communication practices, of a discourse, of a discursive struggle, of a culturally situated message, of means and meanings of a community's communication, of a culturally discursive speech code. Each conceptual framework, then, as each program of research, offers not just a way of understanding a phenomenon in the world, but offers a way of accounting for that phenomenon. In this way, communication is not just the topic of concern, or a description of a social and cultural process, but offers a way of accounting for that concern and those processes.

BY WAY OF CONCLUDING

The study of communication of course has many varieties and flavors. We think this is a good and productive sign. We lament not being able to offer a fuller menu of offerings here for there are many worthy candidates. As mentioned in our Introduction, certainly there are other approaches and scholars which deserve as careful consideration as those we have discussed here. And for sure there are many who warrant as serious consideration as those discussed in detail here. Nonetheless, in the five programs of research we reflected upon, we find at least five distinctive qualities in communication research. These involve conceptualizing personal and social lives as discourses, pursuing crucial social problems as communication phenomena, probing those phenomena, including health, in large-scale data-based research studies, employing a methodology which keeps communication in view when designing information campaigns, and formulating accounts of cultural codes as resulting from communication itself.

We have deliberately *not* discussed these qualities as a quick recipe, or a necessity, or a requirement, or a legislative dictate for all communication studies. We seek not to impose a rigid stamp on the field. We do seek to reflect upon what makes communication research distinctive. The field is of course wide with many rows, several types of soil, each yielding its own plants, and other forms of vibrant life. And there are other fields! Again, we have reflected on just what might be distinctive about our research as *communication* research. We hope the contributions we have gathered here, and our reflections, contribute to a discussion of such concerns. What we have done simply is present five dimensions, a pentad with a purpose, that is, a set of possible topoi for saying what is distinctive in our communication research, as communication research.

INDEX

acupuncture (*Qi*-based) clinic (Ho study), 93–4, 96
alcohol use in pregnancy, community-based media campaign, 22–4, 111

Bakhtin, M., 13, 15, 16–18, 19, 21, 27
barriers in large-scale, community-based research, 61–5
Bassett, D., 100
Baxter, L.A., 17–18, 20; and Braithwaite, D., 16, 20; et al., 17, 23, 25; and Montgomery, B.M., 13, 15, 18, 20; *see also* Braithwaite, D.O.
behavior measurement, 64
Bellah, R.N. et al., 19, 21, 26
Braithwaite, D.O.: and Baxter, L.A., 16, 20, 25; et al., 26; *see also* Baxter, L.A.

cancer information sources, CECCR project, 81, 82–3
Carbaugh, D., 38, 96; et al., 90, 95–6, 98; Philipsen, G. and, 95
Center for Excellence in Cancer Communication (CECCR), 80–4
cervical cancer (HPV) vaccine, 78
'chain of speech communion'/ interdependence of messages, 15–18, 27, 108
childhood obesity epidemic, 78

college students: intercultural adaptation (Hastings study), 91–3, 96; sampling, 63–4; *see also* graduate training
communication accommodation theory (CAT), 59
communication research: *vs* communication science, 73–6; *vs* other disciplines, 14, 33–4, 35, 40, 43, 47, 53, 64–5, 106–7
communication theory of identity (CTI), 59
competing discourses *see* Relational Dialectics Theory (RDT) and applications
conceptualization *see* theoretical perspectives
contestation, 44–5
cultural communication, 58
culture: academic department, 62; grant, 61–2; large-scale, community-based research, 57–60; *see also* ethnographic approach

de-centering the sovereign self, 18
Deetz, S., 32, 34, 40, 44–5, 46–7; and Irvin, L., 36, 46–7
Delia, J., 65
democracy and decision-making, 35, 36, 37–8, 46–7; *see also* politically attentive relational constructionism (PARC)

117